OWLS

Look for these and other books in the
Lucent Endangered Animals and Habitats Series:

The Amazon Rain Forest
The Bald Eagle
The Bear
Birds of Prey
Coral Reefs
The Elephant
The Galápagos Islands
The Giant Panda
The Gorilla
The Manatee
The Oceans
The Orangutan
The Rhinoceros
Seals and Sea Lions
The Shark
The Tiger
The Whale
The Wolf

Other related titles in the Lucent Overview Series:

Acid Rain
Endangered Species
Energy Alternatives
Garbage
The Greenhouse Effect
Hazardous Waste
Ocean Pollution
Oil Spills
Ozone
Pesticides
Population
Rainforests
Recycling
Saving the American Wilderness
Vanishing Wetlands
Zoos

OWLS

BY REBECCA O'CONNOR

Endangered Animals & Habitats

LUCENT BOOKS®

THOMSON
™
GALE

San Diego • Detroit • New York • San Francisco • Cleveland • New Haven, Conn. • Waterville, Maine • London • Munich

© 2003 by Lucent Books. Lucent Books is an imprint of The Gale Group, Inc.,
a division of Thomson Learning, Inc.

Lucent Books® and Thomson Learning™ are trademarks used herein under license.

For more information, contact
Lucent Books
27500 Drake Rd.
Farmington Hills, MI 48331-3535
Or you can visit our Internet site at http://www.gale.com

LIBRARY OF CONGRESS CATALOGING-IN-PUBLICATION DATA

O'Connor, Rebecca.
  Owls / by Rebecca O'Connor.
    p. cm. — (Endangered animals and habitats)
Includes bibliographical references (p.).
  ISBN 1–56006–922–8 (hardback : alk. paper)
1. Owls—Juvenile literature. 2. Endangered species—Juvenile literature.
[1. Owls. 2. Endangered species.] I. Title. II. Endangered animals & habitats
  QL696 .S83 O35 2003
  598.9'7—dc21

                                                    2002003669

Printed in the United States of America

Contents

Introduction

THE UNNATURAL CALL and silent wings of owls have captured the human imagination since the beginning of civilization. For many years, owls were only seen and heard at night, which made them mysterious creatures. Humans imagined what the owls were doing in the darkness and created myths and legends about them. Some early cultures saw owls as wise and kind, but most cultures believed that owls were dangerous or the bearers of bad tidings. Examples of human distrust and fear of owls are found in the earliest literature and handed down from generation to generation in fables and warnings. This ill will toward owls has made survival difficult for some endangered species. In the past humans have persecuted owls, but in recent time this distrust—and even hatred—has turned into fascination. Scientists are now concerned about owl species in decline and in recent years have extensively studied them, trying to discover how humans might help rather than harm them. They have learned that owls are a highly evolved group of animals designed to be excellent hunters in the dark of night.

Unique predators

Owls are unique predators with specialized adaptations, like silent flight or asymmetrical hearing, that other predators do not have. Scientists have uncovered the mystery of how owls fly silently, studying the structure of their feathers and finding that they are different from other birds. Scientists have also discovered that some species of owls have

better hearing than any other predator studied. Their ears are positioned differently in the head than in other birds, and feathers around the face work to funnel sound to the ears. These feathers form what is called a facial disc. With these unique features and their excellent nighttime vision, owls are very successful hunting in the darkness. Not only have owls evolved to hunt in low light but various species have evolved to hunt in a variety of habitats.

A snowy owl lands gracefully at its nesting site. Silent flight is one of the unique traits that sets owls apart from other birds.

Owls are found on all continents and even on isolated islands. They cover most habitats, including deserts, rain forests, grasslands, and old growth forests. Owls have different physical adaptations that help them to hunt in these different habitats. For example, owls that live in the grasslands often have long wings, which allow them to soar over the open habitat as they look for prey. Forest owls

Despite their exceptional hearing, nighttime vision, and unique physical adaptations that make them successful hunters, many owl species, like the barking owl from Australia, are endangered.

have short wings, allowing for better maneuverability as they fly among the trees. Owls have adaptations to help them hunt a variety of prey as well; however, most species prey on rodents.

The endangered owl

Although owls are unique, successful hunters, many species are endangered. Owls are losing necessary habitat to human development, and in some places are being persecuted. Endangered owl populations will be saved only if there is public concern to protect them and a desire to safeguard their habitat. Owl conservationists believe that as more people begin to understand the mysterious owl, the more hopeful the future will be for struggling owl populations.

1

What Is an Owl?

As DARKNESS FALLS and the creatures of the day settle in to sleep, owls wake up and prepare for a busy night. The silhouette of an owl as it spreads its wings and heads for evening hunting grounds is a familiar sight, but there is still much to learn about the nighttime habits of the owl. With over two hundred species of owls existing in the world and perhaps more yet to be discovered, scientists are only beginning to learn about them. The studies that have been done prove that owls are designed to be efficient, effective nighttime hunters.

Owl families

Owls belong to the order Strigiformes, which is divided into two families. Owls belong either to the Strigidae family, often called typical owls, or to the Tytonidae family, often referred to as the barn owls and grass owls.

Tytonidae owls are characterized by their heart-shaped faces, long bare legs, long wings, and short tail. These owls have a finely serrated comb on the inner edge of the middle toe, which is thought to assist in the grooming of their highly defined facial disc. The most obvious difference between these owls and the so-called typical owls is that their middle toe and inner toe are equal in length. There are less than twenty owls in the family Tytonidae. They are a medium-sized owl and depend on small rodents for their prey.

In the family Strigidae are owls that are small to large in size with mottled coloration. They normally have dark brown, gray, black, or reddish plumage. Many of the strigid species have ear tufts, which in combination with their upright stance and spotted coloring, allow them to be well camouflaged against various shades and textures of bark while roosting throughout the day. The strigids normally have round heads and flat faces. Their facial disc is either round, oval, or square, but not heart-shaped like the Tytonidae owls. Strigids also have an inner toe that is remarkably shorter than the central toe. The majority of owls belong to the family Strigidae, represented by nearly two hundred species. Strigids can be found in virtually every habitat and hunt a wide variety of prey.

Both families of owls are designed to be effective hunters in the air. Their differences in anatomy and adaptation make them specific to certain prey and particular habitats. However, they all share the ability of flight and the tools of a hunter.

Designed for flight

The skeletons of birds (also called avians) are specialized to ensure strength and lightness. Like other avians, the bones of owl skeletons are slender, hollow, and filled with air. The major bones have internal struts that provide strength to the hollow bone. Many bones that are normally separate in other animals are fused together in birds to increase the skeleton's structural strength, allowing the bird to endure the stress of flight.

Owls, like all flighted birds, have a projection called a keel on their breastbones. The keel is a deep bone where the flight muscles are attached. It also further strengthens the breastbone. In aerial birds (birds that fly), a great deal of the animal's structure is dedicated to flight. About 20 to 25 percent of the total body mass is comprised of flight muscles.

Although birds do not have forelimbs, many of the bones in the wing are comparable to a human's arm. Bird wings are made up of a humerus, radius, ulna, and wrist.

The bones of owls are slender and hollow, making them light, but their specially fused structure makes them surprisingly strong.

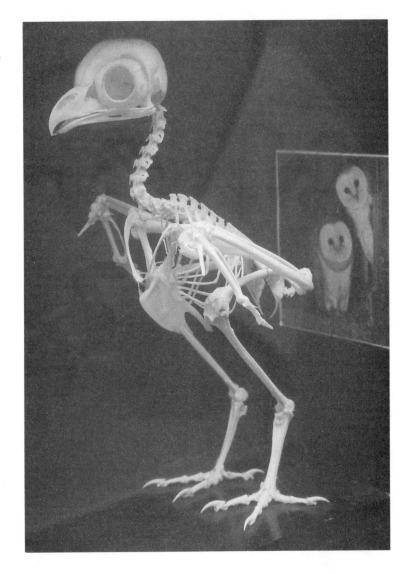

The bird's wrist bones (carpometacarpus and phalanges), although comparable to a human wrist and hand, are much smaller and fused together. Other wing bones have well-defined joints, which allow the bird great flexibility in the way it holds its wings whether resting or in flight. The wrist and hand section of the wings work like a propeller on a plane at takeoff, while the inner area of the radius and ulna give the bird lift whether gliding, soaring, or flapping. Primary flight feathers are attached to the wrist and hand section of the wing, while secondary feathers are attached to the ulna. Feathers are a highly evolved feature on a bird, and birds are the only animals that have them.

Although feathers are designed to be very light, they account for 15 to 20 percent of the bird's total body weight. In comparison, the bird's skeleton is often half the weight of its feathers. Feathers are made up of keratin, the same material that makes up human hair and reptilian scales.

A Newly Discovered Owl: The Cinnabar Hawk Owl

The cinnabar hawk owl is the most recently discovered owl. The first owl was trapped in 1985 and misnamed as a rufous or red phase of another species. In 1998, reexamination of the specimen caused scientists to conclude it was a separate species. In November 1999 the first live specimen was captured in Indonesia, examined, and released. There has been only one other sighting of this species since. Due to the lack of information on the species, its obvious rarity and the continuing loss of habitat, the cinnabar hawk owl is considered vulnerable.

The cinnabar hawk owl is from the family of hawk owls, which have rounded heads lacking ear tufts and long tails and wings. They also have an indistinct facial disc. The owl is small, lightly built, and nearly uniformly rich chestnut in color with a relatively long tail and narrow, pointed wings.

This owl is endemic to the montane tropical rain forest on the island Sulawesi, Indonesia, and can be found nowhere else. There are large areas of virtually unexplored montane forests in Sulawesi, so there can be no certainty of the exact range of the owl. Researchers feel that modern surveys of this land are urgently needed as well as intensive research to find and study this newly discovered species. Scientists are concerned that the cinnabar hawk owl may become extinct before humans have learned anything about this new species of owl and its habits.

They are dead structures and are replaced annually by a process called molting, when the bird drops old feathers and grows new ones.

Feathers have a complicated structure. They consist of a hollow shaft from which parallel barbs branch away on either side. Side-by-side barbs are interlocked by projections and hooks, which are called barbules and barbicels. In this way both halves of the feather on either side of the shaft act as one unit when air flows over it, allowing flight. This is a durable design, but it still requires a large amount of maintenance by the bird. Feathers must be realigned and cleaned on a daily basis.

Owls, like other birds, care for their feathers by a grooming process called preening. Preening is done daily

To ensure optimal flight, owls must realign and clean their feathers on a daily basis.

and much of a bird's time is dedicated to it. Owls generally preen at dusk when they become active. Their plumage is ruffled or shaken and then combed with their claws or cleaned and adjusted by nibbling with the beak. A preening owl also maintains its feathers with a waxy oil that is squeezed from a preen gland at the base of its tail. This preen oil probably keeps the bird's feathers from drying out and becoming brittle. Chemicals in preen oil may also deter parasites, such as mites or lice; fungus; and bacteria from living in or on the feathers. Owls also bathe in rain or puddles to clean and maintain their plumage. If an owl's feathers are not kept in good condition, its flight will be affected, thereby making the bird a less successful predator.

Eyesight

The most obvious feature that makes the owl a predator is its eyes. Just like humans, owls have the forward-facing eyes of a hunter. However, unlike humans, owls have eyes structured to work well in low light.

This does not mean, however, that they cannot see in the daylight. Owls can see extremely well during the day and light does not hurt their eyes. Just like humans, they can constrict their pupils, allowing less light to enter. According to zoologist Claus Konig, "In dusk or in very subdued light, owls are able to distinguish more details than the human eye, but even in bright light they can see better than [humans can]."[1] However, owls cannot see in complete darkness. Although they need some light to see, they can manage with starlight.

Owl eyes have several features that allow them to be effective in low light. The first is their size. An owl's eyes are surprisingly large. According to scientist Paul Johnsgard, the weight of an owl's eyes is "1 to 5 percent of [its] body weight, the same ratio found in humans for the weight of the brain to the body. In some of the larger species, owl eyes are larger than their brains."[2] An owl's eyes are so large, they require a special bony structure, called a sclerotic ring, to contain them in their skull. The sclerotic ring squeezes the owl's eye into place in the skull. The ring

Owls have exceptional mobility in their necks; fourteen neck vertebrae allow them to swivel their necks up to 270 degrees.

causes the eye to be elongated instead of spherical like most animals. All birds have sclerotic rings, but the owls' rings are larger than that of other species. This adaptation allows for the size of the eye, but does not allow for any movement. Unlike humans, owls cannot move their eyes from side to side. Fortunately, owls have a very mobile neck. If an owl needs to see something that is not directly in front of it, it can swivel its neck up to 270 degrees. Owls have fourteen vertebrae in their neck, unlike humans or even giraffes, which both have seven. This, coupled with a swiveling bone structure at the base of the neck, allows for an excellent range of vision, an absolute necessity for a hunter with fixed eyes.

The second feature of the owl's eyes that make them optimal for low-light vision is their structure. Owls have large corneas and pupils, allowing for ease in gathering and processing light. Also their pupils can expand to fill most of the cornea in darkness, allowing more light to reach the back of the eye.

Owls have binocular vision like humans, but with a more limited field of view. Binocular vision is the ability to see an object with both eyes, which allows for depth perception. It is crucial for animals that hunt moving prey. It provides a three-dimensional view, allowing the predator to judge the position and distance of its prey. An owl's visual field is about 110 degrees and 70 degrees of that is binocular vision. In comparison humans have a 180-degree field of vision and 140 degrees of that is binocular. So owls have a smaller area of vision. However, they can easily turn their heads to focus on an object even if it is directly behind them.

Additionally, owls are farsighted. In order to see far distances, they give up some of their ability to see up close. They have evolved to deal with this challenge. They are able to keep track of prey that is being held in their feet by using the stiff feathers around their beak. These sensitive feathers are called rictal bristles and work like whiskers, allowing the owl to feel what it cannot see well.

Owls have three eyelids, an upper and a lower lid as well as a nictitating membrane. The owls can blink their upper eyelid to clean their eyes. They are also able to close their upper and lower lids when resting or sleeping. The nictitating membrane is used to clean the surface of the eye as well as the upper lid. It is a transparent membrane that the owl can see through and often serves to protect the eye from debris while the bird is hunting and flying.

The third feature of the owl's vision that aids in night hunting is the cellular structure of the eye. All animal retinas are made up of two different types of cells: rods and cones. Rods are more sensitive to light while cones define color. Diurnal, or daytime, animals have a balance of these cells. Nocturnal animals like cats or owls have a greater concentration of rods and few cones. Konig states, "Therefore, although an owl's eye is designed to maximise shape outlines at the lowest light intensities, its ability to see colours is very much reduced or even lacking."[3] Because of their eyes' cellular structure, owls sacrifice the ability to see color in the daytime, but can see better than most creatures in low light.

Most biologists believe that owls can see better than any other bird in situations where there is very little light. Considering their specialized adaptations, this certainly seems likely. The ability to see in low light varies among owl species, but those that hunt in the darkest part of the night are certainly well equipped to see their prey.

Hearing

Owls have excellent hearing, which is designed to complement, or in some species, even surpass their eyesight as a tool for low-light hunting. They have developed specialized adaptations that increase their hearing abilities and effectiveness.

Most owls have a noticeable facial disc. The more nocturnal the owl is, the more pronounced the disc's shape. The feathers that form the owl's face are stiff and reflective. This shape is designed to capture and amplify sound, directing it toward the bird's ears, which are hidden beneath the feathers of the outer edge of the disc. Special muscles can change the shape of the disc, allowing it to focus on sounds depending on their distance from the owl.

An owl can hear a range of frequencies similar to what a human can, but its hearing is much more acute. Since an owl's ears are placed on the sides of its head, it is easier for the bird to determine where a sound is originating. To pinpoint which direction a sound is coming from, the owl moves its head from side to side until the sound is equally loud in both ears. Then with one ear positioned slightly higher than the other, the owl can do the same to determine the height the sound is at. When its head is level with the sound, it will equalize in its ears. In this way the owl can zero in on the rustling of a rodent through the grass. Researchers describe seeing owls move their heads until they seem to be staring directly at where they believe their prey to be. Then they launch from their perch in an attack. According to a landmark study by Roger S. Payne, "Barn owls (*Tyto alba*) can locate prey in total darkness using only the sense of

 "Acoustic Location of Prey by Barn Owls"— A Landmark Study by Roger S. Payne

In 1970 scientist Roger S. Payne published a landmark study on barn owls to prove owls can hunt their prey by using only their hearing. Payne set up a light-tight twenty-five-foot by twenty-foot room by covering the windows with masonite and patching any light leaks he could find during the day. Then to test that the room was free of light, he set a sheet of photographic film in the room for one hour and then developed it. If the film had been exposed to any light, it would show up on the developed film. This test showed the room to be free of light. Just to be safe, though, all of his experiments were conducted at night.

Payne put two inches of dry leaves on the floor and set up a seven-foot-high perch at one end of the room. He then released a hand-raised barn owl into the room and allowed it to become accustomed to its new surroundings. In order to watch the study, the room was illuminated by infrared light, which did not allow the barn owl to see but allowed the researchers to view the room.

Once the owl adjusted to its surroundings, the researchers released a live mouse into the darkened room. It took three days for the owl to get comfortable enough to try hunting. When it began to hunt, it was successful on its first try. In sixteen more trials, the owl made sixteen strikes at a mouse at least twelve feet away, missing only four times and by only two inches. The researchers had the same success with dragging a piece of paper on a string across the leaves on the floor. This proved that the owl was hunting by sound, not by smell or by seeing the mouse's body heat.

Payne continued the study and concluded that barn owls have the best hearing of any animal ever tested. Payne's study is now widely referred to by scientists and is the basis for the belief that barn owls have the best hearing of any bird.

hearing, with an error of less than 1 percent in both vertical and horizontal planes."[4] All owls have excellent hearing, but an owl's ability to hear differs slightly from species to species depending on the shape of the face and the symmetry of the ears.

Silent flight

It makes sense that a predator with such acute hearing is able to hunt without making much noise. Most birds' wings are noisy in flight. Wings are meant to resist the air to keep the bird aloft, and the act of feathers pushing against air can be noisy. Since wings move so close to the bird's head in flight, they could disrupt its ability to hear. The flight feathers on an owl's wings, however, have a serrated or combed outer edge, which works like a muffler so that little or no noise is produced when the feather moves through the air. These flight feathers also have a velvety covering that absorbs sound.

An owl's body feathers are loose and very soft. This aids in absorbing sound as well. Owls that have more acute hearing have feathering that allows for silent flight. Owls that are crepuscular, which means they hunt in the evening and at dawn, are not completely noiseless, but are still quiet fliers. Not only does silent or near-silent flight make it easier for owls to hunt their prey by listening for it but their silence also makes it easier for the owl to sneak up on its prey, giving the owl the advantage of surprise.

Owls as predators

An owl's body is designed to help the bird prey on other animals. Owls are strictly carnivores. They share many similarities with their daytime counterparts—hawks, eagles, and falcons. Owls have short curved beaks designed for tearing meat. They are able to move the upper and lower parts of their beak, called mandibles, allowing them either to rip larger food into bite-sized pieces or to swallow smaller food whole. They also have powerful feet with long sharp talons. The owl's feet have outer toes that can rotate so that two toes point forward and two point back.

Their feet are good for seizing their prey with a strong grip and holding on to it once it has been captured.

A burrowing owl swoops down to seize its prey with its sharp talons. Owls are carnivorous and most often prey on rodents like mice and voles.

Owls' hunting preferences

Owls are built to hunt a wide variety of prey. Some owls have long bare toes and legs that are especially effective for fishing. Others are small fast fliers with skills for insect hunting, catching insects like moths, beetles, and crickets. All owls tend to hunt prey that is nocturnal, meaning more active at night. Most owls prefer to eat rodents like rats, mice, voles, and gophers when they are plentiful, even being species specific, meaning the owl will choose to eat only one species of rodent if its favorite type is available in great numbers. Since owls hunt nocturnal prey, they have evolved acute hearing, eyesight, and silent flight to be effective in the darkness. This ability to hunt at night means they do not have to compete with birds that hunt during the day.

What Makes an Owl Threatened?

An owl species is considered threatened when it meets one of several criteria. The International Union for the Conservation of Nature and Natural Resources (IUCN) publishes a list semiannually of animal species that are threatened with extinction on a global level. Most scientists recognize this list as the source for the status of owls and other animal species worldwide. According to the IUCN there are three levels in which an animal could be threatened before it becomes extinct.

The highest level of threat is critically endangered. An animal is critically endangered when it faces a high risk of extinction in the immediate future. This often means that, within a ten-year period, the species has suffered or is facing a reduction of 80 percent of its population. It could also mean that there are less than 250 mature individuals of the species in the wild. The species is considered to have a 50 percent chance of becoming extinct within a ten-year period or within three generations.

The next level is endangered. An endangered species faces a high risk of extinction in the near future. Generally, the species has experienced or is about to experience a reduction of 50 percent of its population in a ten-year period. Populations often number less than twenty-five hundred mature individuals, and the species has a 20 percent probability of becoming extinct in the next twenty years or within five generations.

Lastly, the lowest level in the threat of extinction is vulnerable. A vulnerable species faces a high risk of extinction in the medium-term future. This means a population loss or predicted loss of 20 percent over a ten-year period. Also, the species may have less than ten thousand mature individuals in the wild. The probability of a vulnerable species becoming extinct within one hundred years is at least 10 percent.

Owls are active hunters, mainly because they have little body fat. An extreme example is the barn owl, which has only 6 percent body fat. With low body fat, owls have little energy stored in reserve and must hunt frequently. Smaller owls must eat prey equaling half their body weight every day. Even the bigger owls hunt every night, often eating two or three times. With such a high need for food, it is important that they be masterful hunters.

Owl pellets

Most owls consume their prey whole to quickly eat their meal, which allows them to be less vulnerable to other predators who may try to take the meal away or even prey upon the owl. Feather, fur, and bone are indigestible to owls and are later regurgitated in the form of pellets.

Pellets are one of the most valuable tools scientists use for studying owls. Owl pellets are found beneath their roosts and nesting areas. These small lumps of undigested material reveal exactly what the owl has been eating during the night.

Owls have low acidity in their digestive tract and do not have a crop like many other birds. A crop is a sac that holds food until the bird needs to digest it. Without it, the owl's food goes directly to its gizzard for digestion. Having low acidity means that soft tissues are dissolved in the gizzard, but fur and bones remain. Unable to pass the remains of their meal through the rest of the digestive tract, the owl regurgitates the fur and bone in the form of a compact pellet. Inside the pellet a small skeleton remains, usually with all of the bones unbroken. By looking at the skeleton, especially the skull, researchers can find what an owl has been hunting. The size, color, and shape of the owl pellets vary depending on the species of owl. This is an important tool for researchers who wish to study threatened owls and discover their food requirements.

Disappearing owls

Despite their adaptations for hunting and surviving, many species of owls are declining across the world. There are twenty-seven species of owls currently considered globally threatened, which means they are in danger of completely disappearing from the world, or becoming

Nighthawks and Nightjars

The closest relative to Strigiformes, the order of owls, is not the order Falconiformes in which hawks and eagles belong. The two orders share many characteristics, so it is often assumed that they are closely related. However, recent DNA evidence shows that the order most closely related to owls is the Caprimulgiformes, the order containing nighthawks and nightjars.

Caprimulgiformes can be found on all continents except Antarctica and are only absent from high altitudes and other places with severe winters. They have mottled plumage and are mainly nocturnal. They have a small beak but a large gape, or mouth opening. These birds are able to capture insects in flight with their large mouths. Rictal bristles allow the bird to feel the insects as they come close to its beak. They are excellent flyers with long pointed wings. Like many nocturnal birds, they have very distinctive calls. Scientists use the difference in their calls to tell species apart.

Unlike most birds, the Caprimulgiformes do not have a bony palate. Instead, they have an unusually soft membrane that lines the upper jaw. Some scientists suggest that this membrane is used to feel insects as they enter the mouth, which causes the jaw to snap shut. More recent studies suggest that this membrane is actually an important part of thermoregulation, allowing some nighthawks to nest on the heat of the desert floor. Caprimulgiformes do not build nests like many other birds; instead, they lay eggs by making a scrape on the ground or on flat rooftops.

Caprimulgiformes, though closely related to owls, are separated from them by their short legs and weak feet. They walk awkwardly and are unable to catch prey with their feet the way owls do. They also do not have forward-facing eyes or the asymmetrical ear positioning of owls.

extinct. Many more owls are considered endangered on a federal level since they are in danger of disappearing from a countrywide range. In the United States, the U.S. Fish

Owls eat their prey whole and then regurgitate the indigestible feathers, fur, and bone in the form of owl pellets.

and Wildlife Service decides what species are in danger of national extinction. There are also fish and wildlife organizations in every state that decide what animals are endangered at a state level or in danger of disappearing from small areas of habitat where they were found in the past. By considering population size, researchers can calculate how quickly the population is disappearing to classify the danger of extinction. These organizations generally classify species as endangered, threatened, or of special concern. The International Union for Conservation of Nature and Natural Resources (IUCN), which determines what animals are globally threatened, classifies owls as critically endangered, endangered, and vulnerable, depending on the species. With so many owl populations diminishing, scientists are researching what is needed for owls to survive. The conclusion that many scientists have come to is that what owls need most is appropriate habitat.

2

Habitat Need and Destruction

OWLS LIVE IN a wide variety of habitats. They can be found in rain forests, grasslands, forests, and deserts. Some owls, like barn owls, have learned to use buildings and other man-made structures for nesting and hunting. The survival of an owl species depends on the health of its habitat. Some species cannot tolerate any changes to their habitat and can perish if the land is altered. With their specialized features and need for large amounts of prey, most owls cannot adapt to loss or changes to their habitat or environment.

Rain forests

Tropical rain forests are located near the equator, where temperatures are never lower than 80 degrees Fahrenheit. These forests can have up to four hundred inches of rain a year. Tropical rain forests cover only 7 percent of the earth's surface, yet scientists believe that 50 percent to 90 percent of the world's plant and animal species are found in these forests.

The rain forest is dense with vegetation and trees grow very tall. It has three layers: the forest floor, the understory, and the canopy. Owls in the rain forest depend on the trees for nesting and roosting. They mainly hunt on the forest floor or in the understory, where they can find insects and small mammals.

Twenty-six of the twenty-seven globally threatened owl species are found in the rain forest. Many of them are endemic to small areas of forest, meaning they are found nowhere else in the world.

In general, owls are difficult animals to study, but rain forest owls are particularly hard for scientists to examine. Researchers have a difficult time locating tropical owls because they depend on the sounds the owls make to find them, but the calls of many of these owls have not yet been recorded. Because the rain forest at night is full of noises, it can be difficult to figure out which of these noises are made by owls. There are insects, frogs, and even mammals calling and the sounds can be confusing. The rain forest is also difficult terrain to walk through, especially at night when it is difficult to see. Despite these difficulties, scientists agree that it is important that research is done to discover the needs of rain forest owls before they become extinct.

Much of the endangered rain forest habitat lies on small islands that are inhabited by endemic species. Isolated species that are found in small areas of habitat are more directly affected by habitat loss. These species are confined to the habitat available and generally cannot adapt if their environment changes. One such endemic species is the Madagascar red owl.

The Madagascar red owl is found in Masoala, a peninsula of Madagascar. Madagascar is a unique place full of rare species and a good example of declining rain forest habitat. According to geologists, Madagascar was attached to Africa 165 million years ago. As the continents drifted apart, the island of Madagascar separated from Africa. This separation left all the Madagascar species—plant and animal—to evolve in isolation, making them unique and dependent on this specific habitat. Seventy-five percent of the species on the island, including owls, are endemic. According to researcher Munir Virani, "Habitat conservation is the single most important priority in Madagascar."[5] The red owl is considered endangered because its habitat, mainly the Madagascar rain forest, is disappearing due to human destruction.

Rain forest habitats are also found on the mainland. The habitat of the Sokoke scops owl is an example of one such habitat. These owls are found in the dense woodland areas of the Arabuko-Sokoke forest in Kenya, Africa, and in the foothill forests of the east Usambara Mountains in Tanzania, an area of lowland tropical rain forest. This isolated area is the only habitat where this species of owls can be found and the Sokoke scops owl is unable to live anywhere else. These owls have evolved to depend on the forest. They would not be able to survive if the habitat disappeared.

A white-faced scops owl in the Madagascar rain forest. All but one of the twenty-seven globally threatened owl species are found in rain forests.

Madagascar Red Owl

The Madagascar red owl is a member of the genus *Tyto* and looks similar to the barn owl. It is a red to yellow colored owl, with a finely spotted chest and white facial disc. The total length of the owl is just under eleven inches.

The Madagascar red owl is considered to be one of the most endangered owls in the world. It is endemic to the island of Madagascar, meaning it can be found nowhere else in the world. Until 1994 the owl was known only from eight museum specimens collected before 1935, one reliable sighting of the owl in 1973, and a captive individual in northeastern Madagascar.

On February 22, 1994, two local villagers discovered a Madagascar red owl and took researchers from the Peregrine Fund to the area where it roosted during the day. They were able to trap this owl on October 9, 1994. The owl was fitted with a radio transmitter and released so that researchers could follow it and study its habits. Researchers felt that if they could learn the Madagascar red owl's habitat preferences, food habits, and ranging behavior they could develop a conservation plan for this rare species. They were successful in observing the owl and were even able to observe a breeding pair successfully raise two young. This was the first nesting record for the Madagascar red owl. With the researchers' discoveries, the Peregrine Fund was able to suggest a plan to conserve this rare species of owl.

The Madagascar red owl and the Sokoke scops owl depend on specific characteristics of the rain forest and their numbers have declined due to the loss of habitat. Like most rain forest owls, they are cavity nesters and need specific trees to nest in. They also require suitable perching sites. The Sokoke scops owl is believed to nest almost exclusively in a strong hardwood tree (*Brachylaena huillensis*) that has numerous cavities in it. However, this tree is also sought by woodcarvers and is often illegally removed. Alterations to the rain forest can affect the owl population

---

just as adversely as habitat loss. Scientist Munir Virani states that "The single greatest threat to extant [animals that are not extinct] endemic raptors is from human-induced habitat modification that renders forests or wetland habitats unsuitable for them."[6]

Rain forest habitat is often altered or destroyed by humans seeking food, fuel, and fiber. Land is cultivated for agriculture by slash-and-burn methods, in which large areas of rain forest are cut down and then burned to the ground. Once the land has been cultivated, the rich rain forest soil can be used for agriculture. In Madagascar only 34 percent of the original forest cover remains. Most rain forest habitats have a similar story.

Peruvian farmers burn a section of rain forest to cultivate land for farming. Slash-and-burn agriculture is a significant threat to owl species and other rain forest wildlife.

The rain forest is the most rapidly declining habitat on the planet and scientists are concerned about most species that live there. Studying owls and other birds of prey is a good way to gauge the overall health of the environment. Since predators are at the top of the food chain, a predatory species in decline often indicates that the prey base is declining as well. Researcher J.M. Thiollay states that birds of prey like owls, hawks, and eagles can be "used as 'umbrella species' because their large home ranges and low nesting densities necessitate that any protected areas encompassing viable populations or complete communities protect sufficient habitat and populations of most, if not all, other species in the food web below them."[7] Studying owls could help to save all rain forest species, allowing scientists the ability to suggest habitat conservation plans that include not only owls but all species that live in the owls' habitat. The Madagascar red owl and the Sokoke scops owl currently have more scientific research about them on record than most rain forest owls because scientists have used these owl studies to suggest overall conservation plans. However, there are many more little-known owls that need to be studied in the rain forest.

As humans' need for resources increases, the size of the rain forest shrinks. This is a trend that can be seen in other habitats around the world. Grasslands are one of the most heavily affected habitats as the need for agricultural lands increases.

Grasslands

Grasslands are large open areas of land that receive between ten and thirty inches of rain per year. In terms of annual rainfall, this amount places them between forests and deserts. More rain and the grasslands would become forest, less rain and they would become desert. In fact, grasslands are often the transitional land between the two habitats.

Grasslands contain few trees and shrubs. They are vast flat areas of grass, with larger plants found only near rivers or streams that cut through the land. Wind, grazing

The Sokoke Scops Owl Project

The Sokoke scops owl is a globally endangered species that has only recently been extensively studied. The owl was discovered in 1965 during a U.S. museum expedition. Previously, this owl was entirely unknown. Concerned that the species might disappear before humans could find out about it, the Peregrine Fund assisted with one of the most recent and extensive research projects on owls, called the Sokoke Scops Owl Project.

In 1993 researcher Munir Virani began a study of the Sokoke scops owl. By playing tape-recorded owl calls, Virani was able to study the owls' distribution and population size. The researchers would play the owl call and then record whether an owl responded. Owls responding would be breeding males, signifying a pair of owls in the area. Virani estimated the total owl population at one thousand pairs. By discovering the habits and distribution of these owls, Virani was able to suggest a conservation plan for the species.

The forest where the Sokoke scops owl is found is facing many threats. It is considered the second most important forest in mainland Africa for bird conservation. The threats facing the forest include the clearing of valuable trees for agriculture and to build homes for the growing local human population as well as the removal of certain protected trees for profit. The extensive ongoing research on the Sokoke scops owl shows that what the owls need most for survival is for their habitat to be protected. Virani and the Peregrine Fund believe that ongoing studies to monitor the Sokoke scops owl will be crucial for the species' survival and hope that this project will serve as an example for the conservation of other little-known species.

*The endangered
Sokoke scops owl.*

mammals, and fire prevent woody plants from taking hold throughout the rest of the habitat.

Grasslands appear on most continents and include the prairies of North America, the pampas of South America, the plains of Europe, and the steppes of Asia. The most famous of the grasslands are perhaps the savannas of east Africa, which have more grassland animals than any other area.

Grassland owls depend on an abundant supply of small mammals such as voles for healthy populations and reproductive success. Voles are small burrowing rodents that prefer to live and breed in grasslands. Without the grasslands, voles are not available as a food source and the owl population declines. Voles prefer grassland that has residual vegetation, meaning that it must be burned or mowed every three to five years. Grassland fires are a natural part of the habitat's cycle. However, because of human encroachment and danger to homes, fires are often avoided or extinguished quickly. This practice of stopping fires leaves the grasses unsuitable

Short-eared owls are a species of grassland owl that nests on the ground in depressions that are concealed by the surrounding vegetation.

to the voles, which live within the roots of the plants. Without the voles, owl populations die off or move on.

For example, the short-eared owl is so dependent on a healthy prey base of voles that if the vole population declines, owls will leave the area. The local occurrence of this nomadic species is unpredictable and based on the amount of voles in the habitat. Scientists have found that they can judge the health of the rodent population in the grasslands by monitoring the owls.

Besides providing prey species, grasslands must also contain proper nesting and perching areas for the grassland owls. Short-eared owls nest on the ground in depressions concealed by vegetation. They are one of only a few owl species that builds a nest. These owls need the proper grasses to conceal their nest and young to ensure reproductive success. Unlike the barn owl that will use human-supplied nest boxes, the short-eared owl is completely dependent on available nest sites.

Barn owls need nesting hollows near their hunting habitat, which explains their affinity for barns and silos. As grasslands and nearby stands of trees are cleared to make room for agriculture, barn owls lose their habitat. Barn owls have adjusted, however, finding excellent nesting sites within man-made buildings. In the past, farmland has often had corridors of grassy areas around growing crops and areas of overgrown land that is resting before planting the next crop. These areas make excellent hunting grounds for the barn owls. However, as agricultural practices have changed, these grassy areas have disappeared. Modern fertilizers allow crops to be planted every season without resting the soil and farmers mow and poison strips of overgrown land.

In England, the loss of suitable habitat due to agriculture has greatly affected the population of barn owls. Currently, there are thought to be only four thousand pairs of the barn owl in England and the owls are considered to be locally endangered.

In the United States the barn owl population is diminishing in the grasslands as well. The rich soils of the grasslands make them ideal for farming, and much of the

Because their natural habitat has diminished, barn owls have resorted to using man-made buildings such as barns for nesting.

original habitat has been converted to farmland. This continued loss of habitat has been linked with the decline of grassland owls. In the Midwest much of the grassland habitat has been converted for farming.

Grasslands are also disappearing due to ranching and grazing livestock. Ranchers use grasslands as pasture, allowing cattle to wander and feed themselves. This can be detrimental to the existing grasslands if the cattle are not moved frequently. When livestock is allowed to overgraze, or eat the grasses all the way to the roots, voles lose suitable habitat because they live within the roots of the grasses. When overgrazing affects vole populations, owl populations are affected as well.

Other habitats are also being changed to suit human needs and in turn become unsuitable for the survival of owls. Farming and ranching often require changing or destroying existing habitat, but humans use land for other purposes as well. The development of office buildings, warehouses, and factories also changes habitat. In the desert, habitat is quickly being developed into industrial areas.

Deserts

Deserts are habitats that receive less than ten inches of annual rainfall, have an evaporation rate that exceeds precipitation, and, in most cases, have a high average temperature. Because there is little moisture in the soil and the atmosphere has only 10 to 20 percent humidity, most of the sunlight penetrates to the desert floor. This means that daytime temperatures can be exceedingly high. Because there is little vegetation and trees to retain the heat, at night, the ground radiates the heat back into the atmosphere. So despite the warmth of the day, nighttime temperatures can reach freezing.

About one-fifth of the land surface on the world is desert. Deserts can be found on all continents and include habitats in China, North and South Africa, the Middle East, Australia, South America, and southwestern North America.

Desert owls have evolved to deal with the harshness of a desert environment. With few places to perch and nest, some species like the ferruginous pygmy owl depend on cactus for nesting hollows. The burrowing owl has even evolved to nest in holes in the ground. Desert owls must be able to withstand the high temperatures of the day and the extreme cold of the night. They also must be able to adjust to the lack of water. Desert owls like the ferruginous pygmy owl depend on desert riparian areas, which is land surrounding waterways like streams. Unfortunately, this same lush land is an oasis to human beings as well.

In the United States, the desert is quickly being converted into land for new homes and is disappearing into urban sprawl. According to writer Jeffrey P. Cohn, "The combination of exotic natural areas, year-round warm weather, and little rain has helped fuel an influx of people into Arizona that has increased the state's population by 40 percent since 1990. Tucson alone has grown from a mere

250 people in 1865 to 486,000 in 2000, up 20 percent just in the last decade."[8] In these areas the locally endangered ferruginous pygmy owl is disappearing.

The ferruginous pygmy owl is dependent on desert habitat, especially the riparian areas. As people build homes in these areas, the owl loses habitat. Even where these areas are left undeveloped, rivers, creeks, and washes have dried up due to the pumping of groundwater for nearby developments. As the vegetation dies off, the pygmy owls are left without suitable nesting sites. The small birds that the owls hunt also disappear as the land dries up. Without available prey, the owls cannot survive.

In California as well, desert habitat is quickly being converted into building sites for condominiums and office buildings. As the land is converted into industrial areas, plant and animal life begins to disappear. Scientists have noted a significant loss in the population of burrowing owls in these open California desert and dry grassland areas. The burrowing owls nest in tunnels made by mammals, such as ground squirrels or prairie dogs. They prefer burrows with sandy soil and are well suited to the desert. Although they need these burrows to nest in, they also need open areas of land to hunt on. According to writer Bob Holmes, "Ironically the open space is about the only thing that the owls need to survive. [They] seem quite content to nestle up against even the busiest human activities."[9] However, even these small areas of open hunting ground are being swallowed up by construction.

As human development continues in areas including deserts and grasslands, the need for building materials increases. The demand for lumber has greatly affected the old growth forests because the trees in these forests are being harvested for their wood.

Old growth forests

Old growth forests are defined by physical and structural characteristics that develop with age. They have a larger gap in the canopy formation, which is the area where the tops of the trees join together; a larger abundance of dead

38

trees and logs; and a greater abundance of very large and old trees when compared with younger forests. On the west coast of North America, old growth forest is defined as being older than 250 years. Coastal forests can be even older, because they rarely have fires and thus have more time to develop complex structural characteristics. These forests can be four hundred to five hundred years old.

These ancient forests are important for biological diversity. They have had more time for the colonization of rare and sensitive plant species. Given time and left undisturbed, plants are able to grow and disperse seeds throughout the forests. Old growth forest also may harbor previously unknown species in undisturbed areas. In some parts of the world, areas of old growth forest remain unstudied, and scientists feel this makes research and preservation of the forest all the more important.

Burrowing owls nest in tunnels created by small mammals like squirrels and prairie dogs, and are well suited for desert habitats.

The Burrowing Owl

The burrowing owl is considered to be a species of special concern in the United States. This tiny owl is found in open, dry grasslands, deserts, plains, and prairies. They may also inhabit areas of land that have been modified by humans. Burrowing owls can sometimes be found in golf courses, cemeteries, airports, and vacant lots within residential areas. Although they can be found in a few different habitats, they have specific requirements for the habitat that they live in.

In order for burrowing owls to successfully hunt and breed, they must have a large open area where the terrain is gently rolling or flat. The most critical feature that the owls require is the abundance of active small mammal burrows in the habitat.

The burrowing owl is well adapted to the severe weather of habitats like the desert. Studies have shown that the owl can live in habitats where the daily temperature exceeds its own body temperature. The burrowing owl is able to dissipate all excess body heat by a panting process called gular flutter. The owls have also been found to have feathers that are slightly different depending on the season of the year. The feathers that the owls grow during the winter are better able to absorb the heat of the sun. Despite the owl's ability to share habitat with humans and live in even the harshest environments, the species is declining all over the United States.

Researchers believe that the biggest threats to the burrowing owls are the loss of habitat, reduced burrow availability due to the eradication of burrowing mammals, and pesticides. Researchers state that to stop the decline of the burrowing owl, humans will have to address these threats to the species.

Scientists also believe that old growth forest should be preserved because the endangered species that live there cannot live anywhere else. The age of the forests has allowed them to develop into a specific habitat, which in turn is responsible for sustaining rare and sensitive species. Research has shown that some species, like the spotted owl in the United States, cannot exist without the old growth forest.

In Australia as well, many animals are dependent on this particular type of habitat. In Western Australia, old growth forests comprise mainly eucalyptus trees, which are hollow-bearing trees, meaning that as they age, they naturally produce hollows. In Australia, many of the native owls depend on these hollows, not only for nesting, but also for supporting the species they prey upon. Owls like the powerful owl and barking owl prey on sugar gliders and possums. All of these species need hollows for nesting.

The owls that live in these forests are particular about their nesting hollows. It is estimated that suitable hollows for Australia's powerful owl do not form, even in the fastest growing eucalyptus, until they are at least 150 to 200 years of age.

The larger owls like the powerful owl also require a great deal of habitat. According to researcher Richard H. Loyn, "Large forest owls pose special challenges to forest managers because they are top predators, with large home ranges and complex habitat requirements. Some owl species may need extensive areas of old forest within their home range, as reported for sooty owls in Australia and northern spotted owls in North America."[10]

Like the rain forest owls in Africa and Madagascar, researchers agree that these large owls of the ancient forest are the best indicator of the overall health of the ecosystem. Researcher Loyn states that "The implication is that they are the species with the most demanding requirements, and if they are conserved many other species will be well-conserved also. This fits the concept of large owls as umbrella species."[11]

Conserving these species has come into conflict with industry in the last few decades. The old growth trees used by owls for nesting are very profitable to the logging industry. Researcher Christine Moen points to the fact that because the spotted owls have such large home ranges, "the forest within an owl territory may contain millions of dollars in potential lumber products."[12] With so much money and the livelihood of many loggers at stake, owl conservation and industry need to reach an agreement to preserve the forest.

To date, a tremendous amount of the world's old growth forest has been logged. In Victoria, Australia, 65 percent of the forest cover has been cleared since European settlement in 1788. Forest that has been logged may take hundreds of years to return to its natural state. Even if nesting

The greatest threat facing the global owl population is loss of habitat. Conservation efforts are vital in order to protect endangered owls.

hollows can be found in the new forest, smaller owls that hunt the forest floor have difficulty hunting because the thick regrowth covering new forest floor hides their prey. Also these ancient forest owls have a slow reproductive rate and a difficult time repopulating when their numbers are threatened. If they cannot find suitable nesting sites or sufficient amounts of prey, owls will not breed.

Owls need habitat

In the last twenty years, researchers have begun focusing on what sort of habitat is needed to ensure the survival of various owl species. With their silent flight and nocturnal habits, this is no easy task. Owls are difficult to find and study in the dark, so it is not easy for scientists to gather information about their needs. Still, these studies are crucial to the future of all owls. Many owls are threatened globally as well as locally and their biggest challenge is the loss of habitat.

Although there are many organizations supporting the conservation of the owls, many people still distrust and misunderstand owls. It is important to the survival of endangered owls that attitudes change and that the owl projects win public approval. Without concern from the public, it is doubtful that habitat will be set aside for owl preservation.

3

Humans and Owls

LIKE MOST ANIMALS that are currently in danger of extinction, endangered owls depend on a change in human attitudes and practices for their survival. Although a few human cultures have some fondness for owls, for the most part, superstitions—which are based on misunderstandings and fear of the unknown—have given owls a bad name. Both love and hatred of owls have contributed to the persecution of the birds in the wild.

Misunderstood owls

With their nighttime habits and predatory nature, owls have instilled fear in many cultures and have gained a reputation as dangerous creatures. Many myths that surround owls are based on the fact that they are nocturnal. To humans, especially in primitive cultures, the night is mysterious. The world at night is filled with things that humans cannot see and sounds that cannot be understood. All cultures develop myths around the dangers that lurk in the darkness and tell them to their children to keep them near and safe. The owl, which inhabits this mysterious terrain, is automatically grouped with the dangers of the night. Although owls pose little threat to human beings, the owl's silent ghostlike flight and eerie call only help to reinforce fear in humans.

References to owls as messengers of doom and companions to evil are common in literature. A Bible verse from Leviticus 11:13–17 warns that owls are not to be eaten because they are an "abomination among fowls." Isaiah

14:20–21 speaks of owls living in the ruins of Babylon, implying they are symbols of imminent destruction. In William Shakespeare's *Julius Caesar,* owls foretell the murder of Caesar. The call of an owl is generally thought to mean that something terrible is about to happen.

Owls are often associated with the evildoings of people as well. The witches in Shakespeare's *Macbeth* used owl parts in their cauldron of witches' brew. Owls were considered a witch's familiar, which is an animal that does a witch's evil work, and thought to be associated with the devil.

The symbol of the owl has been used to instill fear in enemies and placed on the banners of warring rulers. Mongol invader Genghis Khan was thought to be protected by an

Throughout history, many cultures have associated owls with evil or danger. This menacing Indian ornament was used to signify the tribe's importance and to intimidate enemies.

owl. An owl once perched above Genghis Khan while he hid from enemies in a thicket of bushes. Although the khan's enemies saw the owl perched above the bush, they moved on without further inspection, thinking that an owl would not sit above a hidden man. The khan believed that this owl chose to protect him. Thereafter, men who followed the khan into battle wore owl plumes in their helmets to symbolize the owl's protection.

The mysterious ways of owls have led many cultures to form superstitions about the various parts of an owl and how to use them. In India owl flesh is considered to be an aphrodisiac. It is also believed that eating owl eyes will allow you to see in the dark. To the English this same ability was once thought to be gained by eating charred and powdered owl eggs. In many parts of Europe, owl eggs are considered to be a cure for alcoholism. An old Yorkshire belief states that owl soup will cure whooping cough. Because of such beliefs, owls have suffered from human persecution for centuries.

Owl persecution

Although owl folklore seems outdated, many cultures still dislike and persecute owls. Researchers Paula Enriquez and Heimo Mikkola conducted a survey in 1997 in Costa Rica, Central America; and Malawi, Central Africa; showing that some cultures still persecute owls because of superstitious beliefs. Enriquez and Mikkola stated that: "In Costa Rica, every sixth, and in Malawi, every fourth [person] interviewed knew somebody who had killed or sacrificed an owl or owls."[13] In Costa Rica 55 percent of the people interviewed have superstitious beliefs about owls, and over 90 percent in Malawi have strong superstitious beliefs. Upon further questioning, the researchers found that the owls are killed for a variety of reasons. In Costa Rica the owls are occasionally killed because they are thought to be detrimental, killing livestock or pets. Sometimes they are killed because of superstitions. In Malawi there seems to be little mercy for owls. They were often killed for fun, to be eaten, because they made too much noise, or to be used for magical purposes. However, the majority of the owls were killed to avoid bad omens. Such strong superstitious beliefs may have developed because these villages are in heavily deforested areas where the only remaining wooded areas are graveyards. These graveyards make good hunting and perching territory for owls. Enriquez and Mikkola state that: "Owls use graveyards for breeding, calling and daytime roosting. As a result, people are meeting owls more and more often in graveyards, thus reinforcing their strong belief that owls are connected with death."[14] The researchers concluded that educating

The mysterious ways of owls have made them the target of fear, superstition, and persecution throughout history.

people about owls is crucial. If local people were taught the truth about the habits of native owls, perhaps they would realize that the superstitions and myths surrounding owls are groundless.

Owls have also been killed because their hunting skills are blamed for negative effects on farms and agricultural centers. On several occasions, owls in Costa Rica and Malawi were killed for eating chickens raised by the local people. Farmers in other countries have blamed owls for problems with their livestock and have killed them as well. In Russia, the Eurasian eagle owl has even been persecuted by the government, which used them as a scapegoat for food shortages. According to author Mykola Rud, "The eagle owl faced especially difficult times with the rise of communists. To explain the food shortages that often accompanied the regime, the government created enemies which could be blamed for any disaster."[15] Scientists were pressured into writing studies that showed the eagle owl to be a pest. Since the 1960s the eagle owl has been a threatened species in the Ukraine mainly due to this campaign of misinformation.

Not all human feelings toward owls are negative, as shown by many stories that describe owls as wonderful companions. The "wise old owl" has become a common saying in the English language. The owl has characteristics that people see as similar to humans. For example, the owl's facial disc looks a bit like cheeks on a broad head that is shaped similar to a human's face. Owls also have forward-facing eyes and a beak that looks like a human nose when covered with feathers. These features have led people to believe that they are humanlike and clever. An owl accompanied Athena, the Greek goddess of wisdom, and also Merlin the wizard in the tales of King Arthur. Despite this positive view, they are no more intelligent than other birds of prey. Still, their mysterious ways and interesting adaptations capture the human imagination. Ironically, even these positive feelings toward owls add to their persecution. Admirers of owls occasionally wish to keep them as pets or as hunting companions, taking them illegally from the nest at a young age. In some countries there is a black market for owls and nestlings are stolen for profit. Other acts of admiration can also cause the owls harm. Amateur researchers and photographers sometimes inspect nests out of curiosity or to photograph the young owls. Although this seems harmless, most species of owl will abandon a nest if it is greatly disturbed, leaving their young to starve. It is for these reasons that in the United States, endangered owl nesting sites are protected and laws restrict activity around them. Sometimes, however, the laws that protect the owls also further their demise.

Owls or development?

In the 1990s when loggers began to lose their jobs and livelihood due to the protection of the spotted owl–inhabited forests, sentiment toward the owls grew increasingly negative. Bumper stickers stating "Save a logger, eat an owl," were not uncommon. These same feelings of ill will could occur toward other owls as they become endangered if public relations are not handled carefully.

Populations of the small ground-dwelling burrowing owl in California are declining drastically and in danger of receiving similar treatment. If the species is put on the endangered species list, it could halt development in California. If construction in owl-inhabited areas is stopped, many people will lose money or be out of jobs causing large-scale economic repercussions. The burrowing owl's defenders worry that listing the owl could cause more harm than good to the species. If landowners see the owl as their enemy, it would be easy for several angry individuals to exterminate the offending population of owls. The bird's habit of sitting in plain sight during the day and only making short flights makes them extremely vulnerable. Biologist David DeSante points out that, "A couple of guys with a .22 [rifle] and a pickup truck could probably eliminate most of the birds in the state."[16] DeSante believes that listing the burrowing owl as endangered "will make the spotted owl controversy seem like peanuts."[17] It seems that the best way to protect the owls is with good

The Loggers' Story

The spotted owl is at the center of one of the most famous and controversial conservation efforts to date, and those most affected are the loggers who lost their jobs when forests became protected for the sake of spotted owl conservation. The little town of Sweet Home, Oregon, was hard hit by federal and state logging restrictions.

The federal government restricted logging in a two-thousand-acre radius around known spotted owl nests, requiring that five hundred acres of the largest trees in that zone be left uncut, and prohibited logging within seventy acres of a nest. The Sweet Home ranger district of nearly two hundred thousand acres produced 86 million board feet of lumber annually in the 1980s, but with the new restrictions the district produced half that amount in 1992. Small family-owned timber businesses closed their doors and large companies scaled down. Hundreds of people lost their jobs.

The community of Sweet Home changed drastically. There were no longer timber jobs for unskilled workers. Mill workers and loggers retrained for jobs in other industries, but often found themselves in low-paying entry-level jobs. Workers could not support their families on such wages. Many loggers found themselves struggling to keep up with bills and hold on to their homes. As the county, city, and local government agencies lost revenue from timber, it became difficult to fund normal operations. So the agencies raised property taxes to try to keep functioning. This was yet another hardship on the Sweet Home community.

Realizing there was a need to represent the interests of loggers and mill owners in the environmental crisis, the communities affected by the logging restrictions joined together. A lawsuit was filed on behalf of the Sweet Home community against the secretary of the interior and the director of the U.S. Fish and Wildlife Service, but was lost four years later.

The Forest Service has since funded many projects to relieve the impact of new timber regulations. A rural community assistance program was created to funnel thousands of dollars into community investment projects designed to diversify means of income and to support the future of the people. The citizens of Sweet Home have also had some success in developing their own strategic plan for improving their economy.

Sweet Home still struggles for economic recovery. Battles between communities and the Forest Service still rage on in court. The question remains on where agencies should draw the line between protecting species like the spotted owl and recognizing human needs.

public relations and educational programs. Consequently, some owls have become "ambassadors" for their species in the work of educating humans.

Owl ambassadors

Rehabilitators, conservation educators, and zookeepers agree that the best way to interest the public in an endangered species is to introduce people to an animal that needs their help. In one such program a burrowing owl in Palo Alto, California, named Sunshine makes appearances to lobby for his species' cause. Sunshine was found on a golf course after ingesting rodenticide. (Rodenticides are chemical poisons used to kill rodents.) He is blind due to the poisoning and therefore cannot return to the wild. Writer Pete Salmansohn states that "When Sunshine isn't lobbying, he's usually out with one of the humane society's professional educators, visiting more than 25,000 elementary school students a year, persuading them with a friendly, yet non-seeing stare that burrowing owls are in trouble and need everyone's help."[18] Sunshine is brought to many public places so that people can see what they are being asked to save and understand what can happen to owls that are poisoned by humans.

The Humane Society isn't the only group that uses owl ambassadors for public education. Zoological institutions and conservation projects also use owls to educate the public about the benefit of owls and the need for their conservation. Outreach programs take owls to schools, believing that educated children will grow into understanding adults who will have an interest in the plight of endangered species. A great gray owl named Lady Grayl served as an example of owl ambassadors at the Second International Symposium on the Biology and Conservation of Owls in Manitoba, Canada. The owl was cared for by Dr. Robert Nero and used for education, research, and fund-raising. Merlin Shoesmith, the assistant deputy minister of Manitoba Natural Resources, stated, "In addition to making numerous public appearances during our National Wildlife Week celebrations, Lady Grayl has given presentations in more than 150 schools throughout

50

A raptor specialist educates a group of curious students about owls and the importance of conservation.

the province, thus capturing the hearts of many Manitobans."[19] By 1997, Lady Grayl had been used for educating the public for thirteen years. Shoesmith also pointed out that Nero's public relations work with Lady Grayl had brought the great gray owl species into the public eye and played a role in the owl being selected as the official provincial bird in Manitoba. Getting children excited about conservation is perhaps the best hope for humans to learn how to live in harmony with wildlife.

Free-flight presentations

Some educators take the human interaction with owls one step further with free-flight presentations, in which nonreleasable rehabilitated owls and captive-bred owls are trained to fly over an audience. People can be told that owls fly silently; however, when an owl flies just above

Owls in Falconry

Falconry is the ancient art of training birds of prey like falcons, hawks, and even owls to hunt game for their owners. Falconry dates back at least four thousand years. The sport has a rich history in times before firearms were invented. Hunting with birds of prey for food is not as efficient as other modern forms of hunting, but four thousand years ago it was an effective way to get a meal. Some cultures depended on birds of prey to help them hunt. For example, the Mongols in China have been training golden eagles for thousands of years to catch foxes and other animals. However, as falconry became more popular, it also became fashionable.

Royalty in many countries used birds of prey to hunt game for sport rather than as a necessity to feed their families. In Japan and England, hundreds of birds of prey were kept by royalty to entertain their guests. In medieval England, there were even rules as to which bird you could fly depending on your station in the court. Only kings were allowed to fly peregrine falcons.

Today, falconry is still practiced in England and in the United States, but it is a hobby rather than a means of survival or fashion. There are regulations and standards that falconers must meet to get a license. Falconers must have the facilities where they house their birds inspected and even pass a test before they can get a license. A new falconer must apprentice under an experienced falconer for several years before being able to legally train most species of raptors, including owls. In the United States, all birds of prey, which include endangered owls, are protected and without the proper licensing it is illegal to own one or even to have feathers from one of these birds.

their heads noiselessly in a demonstration, they get to truly experience silent flight. Other natural behaviors can be showcased as well. In some wildlife shows, barn owls have even been trained to locate objects by sound, demonstrating their keen hearing. When an audience gets to experience an owl performing natural behaviors like flight, it may engage people's attention better, allowing the educator to better teach them about conservation. If people are impressed by the owl in action, they may be inspired to help owls in the wild.

However, there is often some question of whether or not owls should be flown in free-flight presentations. Even for professionals, keeping and training owls is a difficult endeavor because owls can be very difficult to train. Some educators worry that this sort of presentation may encourage untrained people to try keeping owls on their own, thinking they would be as well behaved as the owls they saw flying in the presentation. However, owls in education programs are worked with and trained for many hours daily to be good demonstration birds. Most individuals do not have that sort of time to invest in their own animals.

There is also a question of whether or not certain species of owl should even be trained for free-flight shows. In order to be trained, the owl needs to be raised with humans and imprinted on people, which means they would think of humans as their own kind and not know how to interact with other owls. If the owl does not understand how to interact with other owls of the same species, it cannot be used in a breeding program. World-renowned English falconer and educator Jemima Parry-Jones states that "Most of the owl species can be trained, but whether or not they all should be trained is another matter. For example, I think it would be wrong to hand-rear and imprint for flying a species of owl that is either rare in captivity . . . or rare in the wild. In this case it would be more important for these individuals to be kept in the breeding population, than to have flying for whatever reason."[20]

Educators agree that free-flight demonstrations can be an effective tool for inspiring the public to support owl

How to Study Owls

Owls can be challenging to observe and study even for scientists. Their cryptic feather coloration makes them difficult to spot roosting during the day. If they are discovered in the daylight, the researcher will find the owl doing very little that is noteworthy until nightfall. In order to study the life of owls, scientists must do their research at dusk or in the dark of the night. Since humans, unlike owls, do not have excellent nighttime vision, researchers must depend on their hearing for research.

Many owl species have been discovered by recording owl calls and noting their differences. Species that look almost identical may have different calls to differentiate them. Owls are most vocal during breeding season, so scientists time their studies to occur during that time. When males are establishing their territory, researchers can follow the owl from perch to perch as it calls and map the boundaries of its territory. The calls and behavior also indicate whether a female is nearby.

If a nest is found, researchers observe the owl's routine to discover its prey selection and breeding behavior. The owls also leave clues about their food consumption in the form of pellets below the nest. However, if amateur scientists wish to study owls, they should be very careful not to disturb the birds, especially during breeding season. Check with the U.S. Department of Fish and Wildlife or other local organizations to make sure that there are not regulations prohibiting activity near the nest. Then choose clear, still, moonlit nights to conduct observations. Owls prefer to hunt on quiet nights when there is little wind and it is easier to hear. Watch out of sight and from a distance with binoculars. Recording owl calls to listen to at a later time can help with research as well.

conservation, but that it must be done responsibly. Owl species that are part of breeding projects should remain in these projects and educators should be careful not to send a message that owls make good pets. Recent media portrayal of owls has made it even more important for educators to explain to their audiences that owls do not make good pets.

Owls as pets

The release of the movie *Harry Potter and the Sorcerer's Stone* before Christmas 2001 caused concern among many animal protection groups, whose members worried that the movie's portrayal of owls would encourage the giving of owls as gifts for the holiday season.

In the movie, Harry Potter owns a friendly snowy owl named Hedwig that delivers messages to Harry. The owl seems to be an excellent pet in the movie, causing great concern in the United Kingdom, where it is legal to buy and keep owls. A snowy owl can be purchased in the United Kingdom for about 400 pounds, about $576 U.S. Several groups voiced concern about the welfare of owls given as gifts. Reporter John Roach states, "They fear that when people realize the difficulty of keeping an owl as a pet, the [owls]—known to be temperamental—will be abandoned to a barn or released into the outdoors where they will likely starve to death."[21] If the owls did manage to survive on their own, they would compete for food with the local population of owls. This could have a negative effect on the troubled population of barn owls in the United Kingdom.

The groups also worried that the movie gave the wrong impression about how owls should be cared for in captivity. Jenny Thurston, a trustee at the World Owl Trust, was concerned about how the snowy owl was featured in the movie. She stated, "We understand that Harry Potter keeps it in a parrot cage, which is against everything we know. That is horrendous. It will foul up people's imagination."[22]

Considering the difficulties involved in keeping and training owls, it could be argued that the best way for humans to enjoy owls is in their natural habitat. However, owls often need to live near humans, which can be treacherous for them.

The popular movie Harry Potter and the Sorcerer's Stone *featured a snowy owl, like the one pictured, as a friendly pet. Animal protection groups feared that the movie would encourage people to buy owls as pets.*

Perils of living near human habitation

Owls are drawn to human habitats because there is usually an abundance of rodents. However, the perils of living close to people far outweigh the benefit of a plentiful prey base. The biggest dangers are poisons called rodenticides that humans use to eliminate rodents. Owls living or hunting near the poisoning site are exposed to potentially poisoned food.

Rodenticides are anticoagulants, meaning they thin blood, preventing it from clotting. They are based on the substance coumarin, which kills by causing the animal to bleed internally. Barn owls are particularly vulnerable to rodenticide contamination since they are often found around farms where they could potentially feed on dead or dying rodents. One rodenticide, called Warfarin, is less toxic to the owls, but over the years, rodents have built up a resistance to Warfarin and more toxic second generation rodenticides are being introduced. An example of the potential effect on owl populations by these second generation pesticides occurred in 1984 when they were used at Malaysian oil palm plantations. According to researcher Iain Taylor, "Within 30 months, a population of 40 barn owls was reduced to two, and many were found dead with bleeding from the external openings of the nostrils, a characteristic sign of rodenticide poisoning."[23]

Currently, scientists agree that rodenticides may become more dangerous to owl populations as pesticide use continues to increase. In a thirty-year study on barn owl mortality, researcher I. Newton found that "In 1993–1994, about one-third of all barn owls received contained measurable residues of one or more [poisons], but only a small proportion of birds (up to 3 percent of the total) contained residues large enough to have killed them. With yet further increases in usage, however, these chemicals could become a more important cause of mortality in the future."[24]

Pesticides are not the only problem that makes life near humans difficult. Owls sometimes drown in water troughs, presumably trying to drink or bathe. Barbed wire also causes problems for owls. Occasionally, an owl focused on the hunt will fly into the sharp wire and get hung up, wounding itself or even dying. Burrowing owls have a particular vulnerability to discing, a process in which a large machine digs up the earth. This is a practice used to remove unsightly weeds from vacant lots in urban areas rather than mowing. Unfortunately, frightened and nesting owls retreat into their burrows and are dug up and killed with the weeds. Burrowing owls are also preyed upon by household pets. These owls are small, fly short distances, and are terrestrial, meaning they live on the ground, making them easy prey

for domestic cats and dogs. In addition, living near people also exposes owls to traffic, a most deadly force for a bird.

In Europe, the most frequently reported cause of mortality of banded owls is collision with vehicles. Birds that are being studied by scientists have numbered metal bands placed around one of their legs so that they can be tracked and studied. When birds are found with bands around their legs, they are more likely to be reported by the public. Of the dead and injured banded birds that the public brings in, a large number are found on roads.

One study conducted in northeastern France covering 190 miles of motorway from November 1991 to December 1995 showed nearly a thousand owls killed by vehicle collisions. Researcher Hugues Baudvin reported that the owls

A dead barn owl caught in barbed wire is a tragic example of what can happen when owls live near humans.

were "not just killed by crossing the motorway, but rather that they were attracted by the voles living in the borders. Not only did they take a risk when crossing the motorway perpendicularly, but also when flying along the route linearly in quest of small mammals. They are mostly hit by the vehicle's displacement of air and die of it or are incurably wounded (broken wing) and finished off by the following vehicles."[25] Owl carcasses are frequently found along roadsides in the United States as well. Roadside habitat is an irresistible hunting ground.

Living near humans can put pressure on owl populations. Understanding of the perils facing owls and public approval are the only things that can ease owls' difficulties. However, it is difficult to survive in the wild even without negative human influence.

4

Surviving in the Wild

Even WITHOUT PERSECUTION and pressures from humans, it is difficult for owls to survive in the wild. Owls have specific needs for the habitat they live in and are affected by even natural changes to their environment. Owls also hunt specific types of prey and are significantly affected by the changes in the amount of prey available.

Owls need specific prey

Most endangered owls only hunt a few specific animals as their food source. They also must hunt nearly every night to get enough food to maintain their health and ensure survival. Owls differ from species to species regarding what prey they hunt. Barn owls and other grass owls have long legs and small feet that are good for hunting voles and other small rodents. The long legs, short wings, and small size of a burrowing owl make them fit to prey on insects. In comparison, the equally small cactus ferruginous pygmy-owl has powerful talons that allow it to catch birds larger than itself. Each owl is adapted to be finely tuned to a particular type of prey, which increases its success rate. Unfortunately, this also means that the owls are greatly affected by changes in their prey base. Therefore, when their prey base shrinks, an owl cannot simply switch foods because they are dependent on the type of prey they are designed to hunt.

In North America, the barn owl diet is dominated by vole consumption. Voles equal slightly more than 71 percent of the owl's total diet when they are available. The

Voles

In North America there are nineteen species of voles. Voles look similar to mice and are often referred to as meadow mice or field mice. They are compact rodents with stocky bodies, short legs, and short tails. Their eyes are small and their ears are partially hidden. Voles have a wide variety of color variations, but are usually brown or gray. An adult vole is $3^1/2$ to 5 inches long.

Voles are active throughout the year, even in colder climates. They forage for food normally at dusk and dawn, feeding on stems, grass leaves, and other vegetation. The voles create runways through fields and turf by eating grass blades and constantly traveling along the same path. These runways are about $1^1/2$ to 2 inches wide and are highly visible.

Voles nest in underground burrows, or beneath the protection of an object lying on the ground. The voles reproduce rapidly, and most do not survive more than a few months. They can live up to two years if they are not killed by a predator.

In North America voles are considered garden pests. They damage turf and gnaw on the trunks and roots of various ornamental plants. Voles also cause crop damage, and cost the farming industry millions of dollars every year. In order to control the numbers of voles, farmers and gardeners often use rodenticides and other poisons. Poisons such as these can be costly and negatively affect the environment, so many people are looking for more natural ways of controlling these pests. Many farmers have found that attracting owls, a natural enemy to voles, can help alleviate their rodent problems, especially in sugar cane fields and vineyards.

abundance of voles, however, is cyclical in nature. Their numbers depend on the weather and on three- to four-year natural cycles. Because of this specific choice of prey, barn owl populations change along with the vole population. When there are more voles, there are more owls. The main cause of barn owl death in the wild is starvation through reduced prey abundance. Barn owls, with the least fat reserves of any species of owl, starve quickly.

The short-eared owl is also greatly affected by vole abundance. Short-eared owls disappear from territories that have low prey density and appear in large numbers when conditions are favorable, making local occurrence of the owls unpredictable.

In comparison with the endangered owls, the great horned owl is a generalist, meaning it hunts a wide variety of prey. Great horned owls share habitat with the barn owl and short-eared owl and also prey upon voles. However, they also catch a variety of rabbits, gophers, and mice. Their ability to adjust to prey fluctuation and to be generalists when hunting keeps them from being endangered. However, when times are tough, the great horned owls will compete with endangered owls that they share their territory with for the endangered owl's food of choice. This can make hunting even more difficult for the endangered owl.

The great horned owl's ability to hunt a wide variety of prey has prevented the species from becoming endangered.

Native species competition

Competing with other animals for nest sites and prey can make survival difficult for owls, especially if the habitat available is modified or shrinking. Stronger species of owls may dominate the available territory, pushing the endangered owl out. Even species that normally share habitat peacefully with the owls may compete for food and nesting areas if there is environmental change.

In the United States, the spotted owl is coming into conflict with the closely related barred owl in its limited habitat. Researchers have noted a rapid expansion of the barred owl's habitat in the last two decades. This is worrisome because not only do the barred owls compete for food and nesting sites but there have been reports of the more aggressive barred owls killing the spotted owls in territorial disputes. Biologist Eric Forsman states, "A decade-long effort to protect the threatened spotted owl may go for naught if the trend continues."[26]

The barred owls are larger and more aggressive than the spotted owls. And unlike the spotted owls, they are not dependent on old growth forests for their survival but can live in more diverse habitats. This means that the barred owl is not as limited to a particular type of prey or nesting site and can be much more successful. The more successful the barred owls are, the larger their population will become, making survival more difficult for the spotted owl. Forsman noted, "We could do the best job in the world of managing and protecting habitat and it may not do anything to protect [the spotted owl]. When these kinds of range expansions occur, one species is going to win and one is going to lose."[27]

Recent documentation shows barred owls and spotted owls breeding with one another and this situation worries scientists even more. There have been sightings of successfully nesting owls where one owl is a spotted owl and the other is a barred owl. The young of two different species are called hybrids and this blending of the two species of owls could have unfortunate consequences. The new hybrid owl may not be able to breed successfully because of its genetic makeup. If a spotted owl chooses to breed with a hybrid, and

the two owls do successfully breed, the young will be hybrids and may not even be considered spotted owls. Eventually the population could be made up almost entirely of hybrids. If this happens it could mean the end of federal protection for the spotted owl, as the Endangered Species Act in the United States does not protect hybrids.

Although the spotted owl may have a troubled future because of the introduction of the barred owl into its territory, other owls are suffering from the disappearance of animals once found in their habitat. Some owls depend on the proximity of other animal species for their success in the wild.

The more aggressive barred owl (pictured) often competes with the spotted owl for territory, prey, and available nesting sites.

Symbiotic relationships

Some owls have developed relationships with other species to further their survival. These relationships are called symbiotic, meaning that one species depends on the other for survival. For example, the burrowing owls in all habitats other than Florida are completely dependent on burrowing mammals for their survival. Ground squirrels and prairie dogs do the digging for the owls who then use these burrows to provide roosting sites, nesting holes, and cover. The mammals also act as guards, inadvertently warning owls in the event of predators. The owls watch their mammal neighbors closely for signs of distress and listen for their alarm calls. If the squirrels or prairie dogs sound the alarm that a predator is nearby, the owls take cover as well. Studies show that burrowing owl numbers can decline within a year if ground squirrels disappear from the habitat. Unfortunately for the owls, ground squirrels and prairie dogs are highly persecuted by humans. Researcher David DeSante states, "When the first [human's] horse stepped into a ground squirrel hole and broke its leg, the poisoning campaign began and it never stopped."[28] Humans try to eliminate burrows from their fields where livestock risk broken legs and from maintained lawns where the burrows are an eyesore. Without squirrels and prairie dogs, the owls are not as well informed of the appearance of dangerous predators and are more easily killed. They also do not have proper nesting burrows and are unable to produce offspring. The lack of these companion ground mammals has had adverse effects on the burrowing owl populations.

Burrowing owls are not the only owls dependent on other species for their nesting sites. The elf owl, a species of special concern in the United States, depends on Gila woodpeckers and gilded flickers to create cavities in cactus for them to nest. The owls are unable to hollow out their own cavities and use previously constructed hollows from other species. If those species were to disappear, the owls would no longer have new nesting sites. This also means that they compete with the woodpeckers and flickers for appropriate nesting.

Elf owls are not the only cavity-nesting owls competing for nest sites. In the Australian eucalyptus forest, all the owls and most of the mammals are hollow nesters. The powerful owl and the boobook owl compete with native mammals for nesting hollows. Competition is difficult in normal circumstances, but in places like Australia, introduced species sometimes make the competition impossible.

An elf owl nests in a cactus cavity created by other animals.

Introduced species

Owl populations can suffer and diminish when other species that are not normally found in an owl's habitat are introduced and change the environment. Introduced species are animals that are not native and therefore do not belong in a habitat. They are either intentionally or accidentally brought to new habitats. Australia is a dramatic example of the effects of introduced species. Introduced honeybees, starlings, sparrows, and mynas utilize nesting hollows that would normally be available to native species. The introduced species tend to be more aggressive and can even take over hollows already inhabited by native animals. This drastically reduces the number of hollows available. However, there does not need to be direct competition with introduced species for owl populations to suffer. Introduced species can negatively affect owls indirectly as well.

The owl most recently affected by an introduced species is the Christmas Island hawk owl, which is suffering from the invasion of an introduced insect. The ecology of Christmas Island, located off the shore of Australia, and even the well-being of the Christmas Island hawk owl is indirectly dependent on the millions of red crabs that are normally found on the island. The red crabs are scavengers and their scavenging habits are important to the overall health of the forest. The crabs are also predators, killing animals like rats that can be dangerous to wildlife. Scientists agree that without the red crab the ecology of the island could be destroyed. However, a species called the yellow crazy ant was introduced to the island between 1915 and 1934 from India. Although originally they seemed to coexist peacefully with the crabs, scientists made a disturbing discovery a few years ago. The ants had established themselves on parts of the shore terrace and from there they were killing thousands of crabs that had arrived to breed. The ants attack the adult crabs, feed on them, and once they start to break down, nest in their shells. The ants also harm the forest, establishing super-colonies that compete for forest resources.

The Laughing Owl—Extinct

The laughing owl was the first documented modern owl to become extinct. The laughing owl was found in New Zealand and received its name from the sound of its call, a descending scale of notes. New Zealanders thought that the owl sounded as though it was laughing.

According to naturalists, the owl lived and hunted in open country. The owls nested in the fissures in rock out-crops or even in caves. The entrances to their nests were extremely small. They lined their nests with dried grass and finely powdered rock or dirt. Breeding in September, they fed their young worms, beetles, lizards, and native rats.

Almost as soon as the owl was discovered in the mid-1800s, it began to decline. Naturalists believed that part of the owl's difficulties was the decline of the native Maori rat. However, the main cause of the owl's decline is thought to be animals that were introduced to the island. Ferrets and weasels were brought to New Zealand to control another species that had been introduced, the rabbit. The ferrets' and weasels' introduction had unforeseen consequences since the predators killed not only rabbits but many other species as well. The laughing owl was a small bird with limited flight and made easy prey for the introduced predators.

The last record of the laughing owl was in 1914. The last specimen was found dead by a woman in New Zealand. Rumors persist of occasional sightings of the owl, but none have ever been confirmed.

The previously stable population of hawk owls is now critically endangered by the decline in habitat quality, which has been caused by the loss of red crabs. The ant is so aggressive and spreading so rapidly that the Australian government is preparing for the complete decimation of the entire wild bird population. The government has long-term plans for captive breeding of these species for rere-lease once it has discovered how to control the destructive ant. In the meantime, the future of the Christmas Island hawk owl looks bleak.

Whether owls are indirectly affected by the problems caused by introduced species or directly affected by competition for nest sites, introduced species can cause owls difficulty in the wild. However, even when there is no competition for nest sites, breeding puts stress on parent birds and affects their survival.

Nesting

Raising young requires specific nesting habitat and an abundance of food, yet even when both are available, the pressure of raising its young makes an owl's survival even more difficult. Habitat is crucial to endangered owls; without it, the owls cannot find nest sites suitable to raise young. When the appropriate habitat is available, their success and clutch size—meaning the amount of eggs that the owl lays—depends on availability of prey. If these two necessities are met, the owl pair may be successful in raising their young, but not without putting stress on both parents.

Most endangered owls, like the spotted owl, are slow breeders and only produce several offspring a year. This means that if environmental pressures cause a decline in the population, these owls are slow to return to their original numbers. For these owls, the availability of food can be crucial. A higher prey base means higher success in raising the owl's brood. The stronger, more dominant chick in the nest is the first to be fed. In times of food scarcity during the breeding season, this may be the only chick that is fed by the parents. Siblings may die and only the strongest chick will fledge, meaning it grows large and strong enough to leave the nest.

During times of extreme food shortage, owls may not nest at all. If there is not enough food available for the female owl to put on fat reserves and prepare for laying and brooding, her body will not produce eggs. Journalist Rick Mooney states that in the case of barn owls, "When voles are scarce, the birds may lay fewer eggs, not nest, or even resort to cannibalism within the brood."[29]

The reverse is also true for barn owls. In times of food abundance, breeding pairs of owls will double clutch, or lay a second clutch of eggs after the first has fledged. Barn owls also lay unusually large clutches of eggs when food is available and can have as many as ten eggs per clutch. If food is particularly plentiful, the owls could lay as many as twenty eggs in two clutches.

Hunting for food to feed so many chicks can put stress on the parent owls. Hunting takes time and energy, especially for a large group of chicks. It can also be dangerous. There are other predators like the great horned owl that may prey on a barn owl that is distracted with hunting. Also, the more an owl hunts, the greater the possibility that it could get injured accidentally. Even a minor injury could make it difficult for an owl to hunt and therefore survive.

Even if food is plentiful and the parents are successful at hunting daily, there are many things that can happen to young owls that are dependent on their parents for survival. In the spring, windstorms may blow the growing

Gray owl chicks hatch in a nest. The number of eggs an owl lays is dependent on the availability of prey.

owls out of the nest. The parents will continue to feed them on the ground if they survive the fall, but on the ground they are an easy meal for predators like foxes, coyotes, raccoons, and even domestic pets. Sometimes predators may find the nests. Snakes, rats, and even crows may eat eggs or newly hatched owls. Even if all the young fledge, it is difficult for young owls to survive.

Difficulties of fledging

Fledging can be very difficult, and birds of prey in general experience a high mortality rate in the first year, as high as 65 to 75 percent. Young owls stay with their parents for a short amount of time once they leave the nest. Then they must learn to hunt on their own. If food is readily available, the young owls will have more opportunities to attempt catching food and learning to hunt. In times of food scarcity, the young owl must be successful immediately. Unlike some predators, which stay with their mother for an extended period of time, learning to hunt and using play with their siblings to hone their skills, owls must hunt soon after they start flying, with little room for trial and error. For this reason, starvation is the main cause of death for newly dispersed owls.

Young owls also must learn to avoid common dangers. Owls can become prey themselves if they are not wary. Larger owls are common predators of smaller species of owls. Many young owls meet their demise in traffic as well. One study done by the Iowa Conservation Department tracked seventeen captive-reared barn owls over three months in 1985. Rick Mooney wrote that "Nine of the owls were killed by great horned owls, three died in collisions with motor vehicles, two perished of unknown causes."[30]

Even if the young owls live long enough to develop survival skills, learning how to hunt and what to avoid, they still may have difficulties with the weather.

Living with the weather

Most owls do not migrate and therefore must survive winter weather and other harsh weather conditions. An

owl's need for food and ability to hunt are affected by the weather. Food requirements change depending on the climate, the time of year, and the bird's activity. For example, despite their large distribution range, barn owls are adapted to warmer climates. Studies on the insulation properties of the barn owl's feathers show that they can maintain their body temperature normally if the outside temperature remains between 77 and 91.4 degrees Fahrenheit. If temperatures reach below 77 degrees, the barn owl must alter its behavior by fluffing up its feathers and crouching. Barn owls have a constant body temperature of 104 degrees Fahrenheit, regardless of outside temperature. If the temperature becomes too cold, owls must eat more food to produce the energy needed to maintain their normal body temperature so that they do not freeze to death.

A barn owl returns to its tree nest clutching a vole. Hunting for prey to feed their chicks is time-consuming and dangerous for the parents.

This can be difficult for the owls because in particularly harsh winters where the owl has a higher need for food there is also less prey available.

Feather insulation is also compromised by wind and rain. Feathers are designed to hold in heat radiating from the owl's body or absorbed from the sun. The effectiveness of the feathers is lessened if they are wet or disturbed by a harsh wind. A barn owl hunting in cold, wet, and windy conditions will quickly lose heat. If the weather is too severe, an owl may be forced to stop hunting altogether. Studies show that long-eared owls reduce their hunting activity in heavy rainfall and give up completely in sleet.

Owls' hunting activities are affected by weather conditions. Long-eared owls hunt less during heavy rains, and stop completely in sleet.

Severe weather can threaten an owl by preventing it from hunting. An owl that is unable to hunt cannot eat and must fast. Fasting barn owls roosting in enclosed areas like barns and cavities can conserve a great deal of energy. However, even if the owl is at optimal weight when it begins fasting, it cannot survive longer than eight days without food. In severe weather the owl will not be able to maintain its body weight well enough to survive for even that amount of time. Iain Taylor noted that at one of his study areas in Scotland, a heavy snow in 1981 cut off a group of barn owls from hunting. The snow persisted and within five days the first owl perished.

It is not easy for an owl to survive in the wild. With added unnatural pressures from humans on owl populations, it becomes even more difficult for endangered owls to survive.

5

Conservation

THE FUTURE OF owls lies in habitat preservation, on-going research, and public support. Owls cannot breed and maintain current populations, let alone increase their population, if they do not have proper nesting and hunting grounds. Scientists are unsure of what many of the endangered owls need to breed and hunt successfully, since many remain unstudied. This makes ongoing research crucial to scientists' ability to recommend strategies to save shrinking populations of owls. However, neither research nor habitat preservation can occur without public support. Once owls gain public support and understanding, the next step is to manage their remaining habitat.

Habitat management

As natural habitats diminish, it becomes crucial that people make altered habitats more suitable to owls and preserve existing habitats for the future. Conservationists agree that the best thing that can be done is to set aside land that has supported populations of owls in the past. If the land remains undisturbed by humans, the owls should manage fine without help. However, humans have an increasing need for land as well. Owl conservationists feel that the next best thing that can be done is to manage existing habitat so that it can be shared by humans and owls.

Need for fires

Both old growth forests and grasslands depend on fires for the habitat's health; however, people worry about nearby fires destroying their homes and go to great lengths to prevent them. In the forests, some plant seeds do not germinate or begin to grow unless they are burnt and periodic fires allow changes to the forest terrain, making different habitats within the forest itself. In the grasslands occasional fires keep native grasses at an appropriate length to support populations of voles, which many owls depend on for a food source. Both of these habitats depend on the natural cycle of fires to keep the habitat healthy and able to support native species. In order to preserve grasslands and old growth forests, scientists feel that carefully

Periodic fires can be healthy for a habitat. Here, a firefighter sets a controlled fire to help rejuvenate a forest habitat.

planned and controlled fires, called prescribed burns, should be periodically started.

Scientists recommend prescribed burning not only to maintain habitat but to keep it from being destroyed. Areas that never burn build up the fuel needed to start an uncontrollable fire. If the forest does not burn, the amount of fuel in the form of dead trees and undergrowth increases. When a fire starts, it could then get out of control, consuming vast areas of forest. An uncontrollable fire burns so hot that much of the habitat is lost rather than rejuvenated. This is a big concern for researchers working on spotted owl conservation in the California forests, which are protected from all fires, because the threat of uncontrolled forest fires started by lightning or human carelessness is very real.

Uncontrolled fires in grasslands and forests can also destroy human homes, so prescribed burns could also benefit humans. However, the public has concerns that even prescribed burns could get out of control and destroy their homes. Without public support, the periodic burning necessary for these habitats will not occur.

Need for water

Public support is also necessary to maintain the water needs of a habitat. Some species of endangered owls depend on riparian corridors of land, which is land that runs on either side of a watercourse, like a river or stream. Riparian corridors are changed and even destroyed when water levels decrease. Human use of water can have detrimental effects on this habitat. Homes near the habitat that divert water flows or extract groundwater for human consumption affect the watercourses and plant life. As people consume more water there is less water in the stream or river. The plants in the riparian corridor that depend on this water dry up and die. The animals that depend on this plant life die off as well or move on to other areas.

Riparian areas support prey species and provide refuge during drought. Spotted owl pairs in California often inhabit these narrow stretches of riparian habitat because prey is easy to find there even in difficult years. The ferruginous pygmy owls in Arizona depend on riparian land for the same reason. However, in the desert where the pygmy owls are found, water is in high demand by humans and animals. The riparian area that the pygmy owls depend on is an oasis in the desert where prey is easily found, but it is also an attractive area for humans to build homes and a source of water in the desert. The riparian water is often diverted to towns or to individual households.

Projects like the Sonoran Desert Protection Plan suggest that humans can live in the deserts and conserve the habitat by conserving water. The plan suggests not building near a watercourse on private property, but instead maintaining it for the enjoyment of the native species that are attracted to these washes and arroyos, which are areas of the desert where water collects when it rains. The plan also suggests planting as much natural vegetation as possible around a desert home. Not only do the native plants attract local species, but they also require smaller amounts of water for maintenance, conserving the water available. In this way natural habitat remains for the declining pygmy owl. If humans can conserve the water available to native species, they can help endangered owls.

Maintaining natural cycles and conserving natural resources is not the only way humans can make better environments out of existing endangered owl habitat. In some places habitat shared with humans can be modified to help the owls survive.

Altering existing habitat

Although much focus has been put on preserving habitat, in some areas altering existing habitat can be helpful to endangered species. One example is the roadside habitat in Europe where the roadside grasses are periodically mowed and kept short, which makes attractive habitat for voles. Because of this practice, there is a high concentration of voles along the roadside. The voles attract a large number of owls, which are then being killed as they hunt along those stretches of roads, prompting researchers to suggest making

A barn owl lies dead on a busy roadside. High concentrations of voles alongside roadways attract owls, which risk being struck by traffic as they hunt.

modifications to the roadsides. Researchers believe that allowing the vegetation to grow naturally or planting short bushes would reduce the owl's roadside mortality. Researcher Hugues Baudvin suggests that altering roadside habitat "would decrease prey availability and lead owls toward other areas which may be rich in prey, but surely less dangerous."[31] Even in areas where owls are not in danger while hunting, some conservation projects are suggesting ways to help owls be more successful hunting.

The Barn Owl Centre in England is trying to educate farmers about methods for making their land more habitable to the locally endangered barn owl without entailing extra expense or labor. Intensive agriculture leaves habitat unsuitable for the voles on which barn owls prey. The Barn Owl Centre suggests that farmers create additional areas of rough pasture if land is not being farmed. They can also create much wider corridors of rough grassland along hedgerows and ditches. The center also asks that farmers not drain or reseed existing pasture or overgraze. All these measures allow the vole population to flourish and give the barn owls a prey base.

There needs to be public concern for habitat to be maintained or modified. Some owl conservation projects have found that to keep people interested in conserving and maintaining habitat, it helps for the people involved to be able to make a living working with the habitat instead of destroying it.

 Operation Burrowing Owl

In Canada there is a great deal of concern over the plight of the enigmatic burrowing owl. The owl is currently considered endangered in Canada and the numbers are declining every year. In several areas the species is facing extirpation, meaning it could become extinct from a historic region.

With this concern, the Saskatchewan-based Operation Burrowing Owl was launched in 1987. It is a successful and nationally recognized habitat conservation program that has the participation of almost eight hundred landowners. The program has four objectives:

1. To protect burrowing owl habitat through voluntary habitat protection agreements with landowners.
2. To increase and maintain the awareness of the burrowing owl as an endangered species.
3. To compile an annual population census of burrowing owls in Saskatchewan.
4. To facilitate research and enhance nesting habitat.

Landowners choose to participate in this program. Participants sign an agreement to preserve the historic nesting area by not destroying the habitat or disturbing the birds. The owls usually nest on grazed pasture and hunt in taller grasses. Each summer the landowners send in a census card or call to report the status of the owls on their property. In return landowners receive an annual newsletter keeping them up-to-date on the burrowing owls' status. Although the burrowing owl continues to decline in numbers, Canadians are hopeful that research and public awareness will save their population of burrowing owls.

Sustainable harvest and ecotourism

Finding ways for communities to make money in ways that do not destroy endangered owl habitat will ensure the future of owl species. This is especially needed in rain forest habitats, where there are currently few ways to make money other than farming, which usually requires the destruction of the rain forest.

To entice people into working with the environment, a method called sustainable harvest is being attempted in many rain forests throughout the world. This is a method where products that do not interfere with the habitat are grown and harvested. Coffee is often grown in this manner. Coffee can be grown in the shade of the rain forest floor without having to disturb the forest. Sustainable harvest is an experimental method of conservation and depends on figuring out a way to become more profitable than slash-and-burn agriculture, which destroys the rain forest. Most crops can only grow in the rich soil of the rain forest after the forest plant life is removed, and this is usually done by cutting the rain forest down and burning the remains. In Kenya and Madagascar, local people are taught how to grow sustainable harvests to save habitat for the Sokoke scops owl and the Madagascar red owl. In both of these places, some other experimental means of bringing in local income are being used as well.

Ecotourism is another effective way to involve locals in conservation and to bring income to the community at the same time. Ecotourism generates local income by encouraging tourists to come to the conservation site for guided tours that do not disturb the habitat. Locals make money by charging tourists for these tours. The local economy also benefits from the money that tourists spend on food, lodging, and other goods. Madagascar is one example of how ecotourism benefits both locals and conservation projects. There, researchers take "birders" to a place where they can sight the radio-tagged rare Madagascar red owl. The birders are able mark the owl off their life list of birds that they have seen, and in return, the tourists donate money to the local Ambanizana Village School. The local

Tourists watch birds in the Madagascar rain forest.

schoolteacher explains to the children at the school the forest's importance in keeping the tourists visiting and their impact on the local economy. In this way the local endangered habitat can benefit the local people, yet be sustained at the same time. The owls benefit indirectly. In some places, however, humans are working to help owls directly.

Nest boxes

Although many breed-and-release projects have proven to be unsuccessful, the introduction of nest boxes and future breeding projects may be ways that humans can help owls directly. A nest box is a box built by humans designed to simulate a place where owl pairs would choose to lay eggs and raise young.

In Malaysian oil palm plantations, it has been shown that barn owl populations can be increased by providing proper nesting sites. In 1988, two hundred nest boxes were erected on a plantation southeast of Kuala Lumpur in an effort to use barn owls to reduce crop loss caused by rats. According to researcher Iain Taylor, "These [nest boxes] were taken up quickly and by December 1989, only 20 months later, 95%

were occupied by breeding barn owls. This must surely be the densest barn owl population anywhere."[32] The example in Malaysia shows that just by supplying the necessary nesting sites, owl populations can be increased.

However, the solution is not always so simple. Research has shown that providing usable burrows for nesting burrowing owls does not greatly benefit the population. Owls nesting in manufactured burrows have a much lower success rate for fledged young than those that nest in natural burrows. Perhaps if more research is done, scientists can design a more suitable burrow for burrowing owls that are lacking places to nest. Another effort that researchers have made is to breed and release owls into habitat where they were once found in large numbers, before their decline.

 Burrowing Owls at Mission College

Burrowing owls are a familiar sight for the students at Mission College, located on a large campus in Santa Clara, California. Forty feet away from a busy walkway, burrowing owls nest and hunt. The owls do not seem to mind the closeness of the students as long as suitable habitat is available.

In 1990, the college made the decision to lease about seventy of its one hundred acres to developers for a shopping mall, some of which was prime burrowing owl habitat. With some persuasion from environmental scientists, the college and the developers agreed to make room for as many owl burrows as possible on what remained of the fields they lived in. The college also agreed to set aside some pockets of land not slated for construction as owl habitat for the next twenty years.

The owls are dependent on ground squirrels for the production of their nesting burrows. To reduce the owl's dependence on the ground squirrels, the college put in artificial burrows. Eight-foot-long terra cotta pipes were buried with nest boxes at the end. Then the college agreed to mow regularly to keep the grass low so that the owls had better hunting grounds.

Most of the school's staff and students are involved with the project either directly or indirectly. The owls seem to have a great deal of support. However, only twelve of the original sixteen pairs remain. Researchers worry that there is only enough habitat to support about eight pairs in the long run. However, students and staff seem determined to give the tiny owls a chance.

Captive breeding

In an attempt to increase the numbers of owls in the wild, scientists take part in breed and release or captive breeding, which means owls are born into captivity and released into the wild when they are ready to leave the nest. Scientists have attempted many breed-and-release projects around the world for owls that are declining in specific areas of habitat. For the most part these attempts have been disastrous, with few of the young owls surviving.

In Great Britain, almost anyone was allowed to breed and release barn owls across the country in the early 1990s without rigid regulation. Unfortunately, with the lack of regulations thousands of owls have been released, more than the existing habitat can sustain, and few have been documented as surviving. The owls that do survive could possibly be competing for food with owls that are already established in the wild. Instead of helping the wild population, the well-meaning breeders could be making survival more difficult for existing wild owls. The English agree that the owls that have been released have not contributed to increasing the wild population.

In the United States, the same situation has occurred with the local population of barn owls. In the Midwest, barn owl numbers have dramatically fallen. Intensive breed-and-release projects have been attempted, but almost all the owls released have come up unaccounted for. Most captive-bred birds perished when released into the wild. Because of these poor results, breed-and-release projects have been discontinued in the United States.

However, the failure of these projects seems to be because of the lack of appropriate habitat, so scientists are hopeful that future breed-and-release projects may be more successful. Researcher John Cayford states, "Reintroduction programmes are likely to be worthless unless steps are taken to improve habitat."[33] If the young owls do not have enough prey to hunt or the appropriate land to hunt on, they cannot survive. Other smaller scale captive breeding projects have been successful. In Europe a reintroduction of the Eurasian eagle owl was successful in some areas of forest from which

84

A breed-and-release project in Europe has successfully reintroduced the Eurasian eagle owl to areas where its population had disappeared.

the species had previously disappeared. Also, there is some hope at Christmas Island for the prospects of a captive breeding project. Once the introduced species of yellow crazy ant has been controlled or eradicated, the Australians hope that captive-bred Christmas Island hawk owls can be reintroduced to a once again pristine habitat. Many scientists feel that as long as there is food available and it is done properly, breed-and-release projects can be successful.

However, owls are dependent on the habitat available to them. Without habitat, the breed-and-release projects will not be successful. Owls need land to thrive and research needs to be done to uncover exactly what different species of owl need in their habitat. Without research, scientists cannot create the conservation plans necessary to save the various species of endangered owls.

Need for research

Without understanding owl species and their status, researchers agree that it is difficult to conserve endangered owls. Researcher Munir Virani states, "For raptors rated as Little Known and at least Threatened, priority should be given to studies that collect the information needed to determine the best course of action to reduce the probability of the species' extinction."[34] Although there are several extensive owl research projects that are currently ongoing, there are many more owls that scientists know little about. Despite the obvious need for studies, finding researchers and money to support the projects can be difficult.

Biologists examine a young spotted owl. Careful study of owls helps researchers develop effective conservation strategies.

Many biologists agree that owl conservation studies can benefit entire habitats and all of the species that live there. Owls act as an "umbrella" species, meaning that a healthy owl population indicates that all of the species beneath it are doing fine as well. If there are problems with top predators in a habitat, such as owls, this is often an indicator that there are fewer prey species and something is wrong with the environment. Studying owls can help researchers discover if other species in the habitat are having difficulties. This is the philosophy of one of the most extensive research projects on an endangered owl, the Masoala Project.

The Masoala Project

The Masoala Project in Madagascar is an example of how extensive research can benefit endangered owls. The project is supported by the Peregrine Fund, which is an organization that believes research is crucial for species preservation.

The Madagascar red owl was thought to be extinct, but when the Peregrine Fund rediscovered the owl, they were able to begin an extensive research project and develop a plan to save the endangered owl. Until 1994, this owl was known only from eight museum specimens and one reliable sighting of the bird in 1973. The owl was rediscovered during an ongoing study to count and record the avian species on Madagascar. Without understanding a species and its status, researchers agree that it is difficult to conserve endangered animals. Once the Madagascar red owl was rediscovered, biologists thought it was important to study the owl species and learn as much about it as possible, especially since the location of its discovery contradicted previous beliefs about the owl's habitat requirements.

When biologists from the Peregrine Fund found an individual red owl on Masoala Peninsula they captured, radio-tagged, and released it for study in October 1994. By tracking the owl, researchers were able to study the bird's habitat use and discover that it was not restricted to the forest as was previously thought, but would also hunt on habitat disturbed by humans. Researchers also discovered that

The Peregrine Fund

The Peregrine Fund is one of the most successful conservation groups in the United States. Tom Cade, while working as professor of ornithology at Cornell University, founded the Peregrine Fund in 1970. The name came from a financial account called the peregrine fund at the Cornell Laboratory of Ornithology. The concern of students and scientists regarding the plight of the peregrine falcon blossomed into an organization with the goal of protecting the species. It was obvious at the time that the falcon was on the road to extinction. The initial work done by the group was to learn how to breed the peregrines in captivity with the hope that they could reestablish a population of the bird in the eastern United States, where it had completely disappeared, and to increase the western population as well. Not only was their breeding project successful, but with the help of other organizations and individuals the peregrine was taken off the endangered species list in the United States in 1999.

The Peregrine Fund also boasts the first successful release of the American bald eagle, which was recently de-listed as well. The Peregrine Fund went on to save the Mauritius kestrel from extinction and continues to support raptor preservation projects around the world. The Peregrine Fund is firm in the belief that raptors (birds of prey) are a monitor of environmental health and that if raptors like owls are protected in an environment, then the diversity of species in that habitat is also preserved.

A rehabilitation aide from the Peregrine Fund uses a hand puppet to feed falcon chicks.

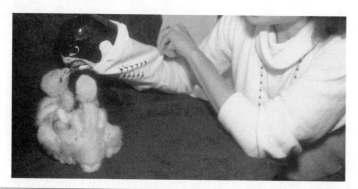

the red owl had hunting habits and vocalizations similar to the barn owl, which could mean that it was often mistaken for the closely related barn owl in the field. Biologists were also able to study the first known nesting pair of Madagascar red owls during the Masoala study and record what was necessary for a pair of owls to breed successfully. The newly acquired information left scientists hopeful for the red owl's future and the Peregrine Fund was able to begin a species survival program for the owl. However, scientists agree that ongoing research will be a crucial part of the survival program.

The Sonoran Desert Project

In the United States a progressive conservation project is taking place to protect the tiny cactus ferruginous pygmy owl in the Sonoran Desert of Arizona. With only seventy ferruginous pygmy owls in the Sonoran Desert area, the residents of Pima County in Arizona found development coming to a screeching halt when the owl was discovered on land slated for new building. Rather than face the prospect of lawsuits and having to get permits for every new development, the county decided to commit to protecting the species. A series of meetings began in 1998 that led to a multispecies habitat conservation plan. County administrator Maeveen Behan, who is in charge of the planning effort, states, "We decided . . . to place biology in front of development. Our goal was the owl's recovery."[35] Pima County chose to achieve higher conservation goals than what federal law defines as a minimum.

Based on recommendations from biologists and federal agency staff and comments from the community, in 1998 Pima County initiated more comprehensive studies on the pygmy owls using telemetry (radio-tracking) studies, habitat assessments, population success analysis, and genetic research. With this extensive research information, the county is able to make more informed decisions about land use. A committee is currently working on strategies for land use that protects habitat but does not completely exclude development. The county hopes the committee will be able

The Cactus Ferruginous Pygmy Owl

The cactus ferruginous pygmy owl is not globally threatened, but it is in danger of completely disappearing from habitat where it has always been found. This has caused a great deal of concern among scientists in the United States. The owl is considered to be endangered in Arizona by the U.S. Fish and Wildlife Service. Recent studies show that there are seventy pygmy owls and thirteen active nests, mostly around Tucson and Organ Pipe Cactus National Monument.

The cactus ferruginous pygmy owl is found in limited areas in North America and throughout much of South America. The North American subspecies is restricted to desert habitats, and can be found in wooded riparian areas of the Sonoran Desert in Arizona.

The cactus ferruginous pygmy owl is a small owl (17 cm, or 6.69 inches) with a rounded head, no ear tufts, and yellow eyes. It has relatively short wings and a long tail for an owl. Its coloration is reddish-brown overall, with a cream-colored belly that is streaked with reddish-brown. These owls also have a lightly streaked crown and paired black and white spots on the back of the nape that suggest eyes.

This tiny owl has recently sparked a large-scale conservation project in the United States, called the Sonoran Desert Project. Arizona is attempting to find ways for humans and owls to share habitat and also setting aside large sections of land for preserves to protect a wide variety of species. If these efforts are successful, the tiny cactus ferruginous pygmy owl may survive and thrive again in the desert.

to propose a plan for land use and a funding scheme for multispecies habitat conservation with U.S. Fish and Wildlife Service approval by the end of 2002. According to writer Jeffrey P. Cohn, "The effort to protect the Sonoran Desert represents one of the most ambitious, ecosystem-wide conservation efforts currently underway in the United States."[36] If the plan is ultimately successful, it could serve as an example for future conservation efforts.

Beneficial owls—changing opinions

As people learn more about the owl's role in the environment, public opinion about owls is slowly changing. Owls were once seen as frightening creatures of the night, but are now being thought of as nighttime protectors of crops and fields. Recently, farmers have come to see the owl's role—especially that of the barn owl—in the control of rodent populations.

The agriculture industry has been taking a hard look at using barn owls to fight rodent populations in their fields and has discovered that the owls can be helpful. Previously, many farmers have thought the owls to be a nuisance, leaving a mess beneath their nests and roosts in barns, silos, and pump houses. Now sugar cane growers and wine grape growers are inviting the owls into their fields with perches and nest boxes.

In Florida, where a large amount of sugar cane is grown, cotton rats cause more than $30 million in damage every year. To help battle this loss, growers spend between five and ten dollars an acre on chemicals to kill the rodents. Barn owls are a much less expensive alternative. Research has shown that a family of barn owls can eat as many as three thousand rodents during the course of the breeding season. With these numbers in mind, growers have looked into the value of attracting as many barn owls as possible to their fields. Barn owls are not territorial and will nest close to one another if food is plentiful. More owls means fewer rodents and less crop destruction. Barn owls have become a farmer's ally, and this change of attitude may help to encourage support in barn owl conservation.

The future

If these projects find success and other research and conservation efforts are begun, perhaps humans can save the endangered owls from extinction. Even in the last ten years owls have generated research and interest. Public opinion is slowly changing as people learn the natural history of these birds—a history that has previously been hidden by the darkness of the night. People are beginning to

Farmers are studying ways to use barn owls, previously viewed as nuisances, to control rodent populations in their fields.

view owls as beneficial creatures and find interest in their future. Owls have recently been portrayed as friends to humans in the media, which has also generated favorable interest. As long as humans are responsible in their interactions with owls, this new interest could be beneficial to many owl species. Owls need habitat and perhaps as people gain appreciation for owls they will set aside and share habitat with these nighttime hunters. Human interest may be exactly what endangered owls need to survive.

Notes

Chapter 1: What Is an Owl?

1. Claus Konig et al., *Owls: A Guide to Owls of the World.* New Haven, CT: Yale University Press, 1999, p. 19.

2. Quoted in Kim Long, *Owls: A Wildlife Handbook.* Boulder, CO: Johnson Books, 1998, p. 91.

3. Konig et al., *Owls,* p. 19.

4. Roger S. Payne, "Acoustic Location of Prey by Barn Owls (*Tyto alba*)," *Journal of Experimental Biology,* vol. 54, 1971, p. 570.

Chapter 2: Habitat Need and Destruction

5. Munir Virani and Richard T. Watson, "Raptors in the East African Tropics and Western Indian Ocean Islands: State of Ecological Knowledge and Conservation Status," *Journal of Raptor Research,* vol. 32, no. 1, 1998, p. 28.

6. Virani and Watson, "Raptors in the East African Tropics and Western Indian Ocean Islands," p. 34.

7. Virani and Watson, "Raptors in the East African Tropics and Western Indian Ocean Islands," p. 28.

8. Jeffrey P. Cohn, "Sonoran Desert Conservation," *Bio-Science,* vol. 51, no. 8, 2001, pp. 607–608.

9. Bob Holmes, "City Planning for Owls," *National Wildlife,* vol. 36, no. 6, 1998, p. 50.

10. Richard H. Loyn et al., "Modelling Landscape Distributions of Large Forest Owls as Applied to Managing Forests in North-East Victoria, Australia," *Biological Conservation,* vol. 97, 2001, p. 361.

11. Loyn et al., "Modelling Landscape Distributions of Large Forest Owls," p. 371.

12. Christine Moen and R.J. Gutierrez, "California Spotted Owl Habitat Selection in the Central Sierra Nevada," *Journal of Wildlife Management,* vol. 61, no. 4, 1997, p. 1,281.

Chapter 3: Humans and Owls

13. Paula Enriquez and Heimo Mikkola, "Comparative Study of General Public Owl Knowledge in Costa Rica, Central America and Malawi, Central Africa," *Biology and Conservation of Owls of the Northern Hemisphere,* James Duncan, ed., Winnipeg, Manitoba, CN: USDA Forest Service, 1997, p. 163.

14. Enriquez and Mikkola, "Comparative Study of General Public Owl Knowledge," p. 165.

15. Mykola Rud, "Eagle Owl (*Bubo bubo*)," *The Naturalist.* http://proeco.visti.net.

16. Quoted in Holmes, "City Planning for Owls," p. 50.

17. Quoted in Pete Salmansohn, "Plowed Under," *Wildlife Conservation,* vol. 96, November/December 1993, p. 24.

18. Salmansohn, "Plowed Under," p. 28.

19. Merlin Shoesmith, "Official Opening Remarks: Manitoba Natural Resources," *Biology and Conservation of Owls of the Northern Hemisphere,* p. 1.

20. Jemima Parry-Jones, *Understanding Owls.* Devon, UK: David and Charles, 1998, p. 119.

21. John Roach, "Harry Potter Owl Scenes Alarm Animal Advocates," *National Geographic News,* November 16, 2001. http://news.nationalgeographic.com.

22. Quoted in Roach, "Harry Potter Owl Scenes Alarm Animal Advocates."

23. Iain Taylor, *Barn Owls.* UK: Cambridge University Press, 1994, p. 242.

24. I. Newton et al., "Mortality Causes in British Barn Owls (*Tyto alba*), Based on 1,101 Carcasses Examined During 1963–1996." *Biology and Conservation of Owls of the Northern Hemisphere,* p. 306.

25. Hugues Baudvin, "Barn Owl (*Tyto alba*) and Long-Eared Owl (*Asio otus*) Mortality Along Motorways in Bourgogne-

Champagne: Report and Suggestions," *Biology and Conservation of Owls of the Northern Hemisphere*, p. 60.

Chapter 4: Surviving in the Wild

26. Quoted in Associated Press, "Endangered Spotted Owl Faces New Threat from Relative," August 8, 2000. www.cnn.com.
27. Quoted in Associated Press, "Endangered Spotted Owl."
28. Quoted in Salmansohn, "Plowed Under," p. 25.
29. Rick Mooney, "Helping a Heartland Hunter," *National Wildlife,* vol. 26, no. 4, 1988, p. 43.
30. Mooney, "Helping a Heartland Hunter," p. 44.

Chapter 5: Conservation

31. Baudvin, "Barn Owl (*Tyto alba*) and Long-Eared Owl (*Asio otus*) Mortality," p. 60.
32. Taylor, *Barn Owls*, p. 252.
33. John Cayford and Steve Percival, "Born Free, Die Free," *New Scientist,* February 8, 1992, p. 33.
34. Virani and Watson, "Raptors in the East African Tropics and Western Indian Ocean Islands," p. 36.
35. Quoted in Cohn, "Sonoran Desert Conservation," p. 608.
36. Cohn, "Sonoran Desert Conservation," p. 606.

Glossary

binocular vision: The ability to see a single image with both eyes.

cache: To hide excess food in a place where it can be used at a later time.

clutch: A group of eggs that is laid in a single nest.

cone: A cone-shaped cell in the retina of the eye that determines color.

crepuscular: Active in the evening and early morning hours.

diurnal: Active in the daytime.

ecosystem: A group of organisms that depend on one another and the environment in which they live in order to survive.

extant: Still in existence.

endemic: Found in a limited area of habitat and nowhere else in the world.

facial disc: The circlet of feathers that encircles the eyes of owls and is used to collect sound waves.

fledge: The time between a young bird flying from the nest for the first time until it is no longer dependent on parental care.

hybrid: An animal that has parents from different species.

imprinted: An animal that has been raised and socialized with humans, therefore not being socialized with its own kind.

nocturnal: Active in the night.

molt: The act of dropping feathers to grow new replacement feathers.

preen: The act of a bird grooming and caring for its feathers.

preen gland: A gland near the tail of the bird, which provides oils that the bird rubs on its feathers to keep them in good condition.

prey base: The amount of prey available to a species of animal.

rictal bristles: A stiff feather that grows around the beak of an owl and acts like a whisker, allowing the bird to feel objects near its mouth.

riparian: Associated with rivers or streams.

rod: A rod-shaped cell in the retina of the eye that is sensitive to dim light, but not to color.

sclerotic ring: A thin overlying bony plate that protects and strengthens the eyeball.

Strigidae: The family that most owls are classified under. The characteristics of this family are a round face and an inner toe remarkably shorter than the central toe.

Strigiformes: The order of animals under which scientists classify owls.

Tytonidae: The family of owls that barn owls and grass owls belong to. The characteristics of this family are a heart-shaped or triangular face, a short square tail, and an inner toe equal to the length of the middle toe.

Organizations
to Contact

Birds Australia
415 Riversdale Rd.
Hawthorn East, VIC 3123, Australia
Tel: 61 3 9882 2622
e-mail: mail@birdsaustralia.com.au
www.birdsaustralia.com.au

Originally the Royal Australasian Ornithologists Union, Birds Australia is involved in bird conservation nationally in Australia, sponsoring projects and public education programs.

The Hawk and Owl Trust
c/o Zoological Society of London
Regents Park, London, NW1 4RY, UK
Tel: 44 01452 502155
e-mail: hawkandowltrust@aol.com
www.hawkandowl.org

The Hawk and Owl Trust works for the conservation and appreciation of wild birds of prey and their habitats through projects that involve practical research, creative consultation, and imaginative education.

Peregrine Fund
5666 W. Flying Hawk Lane
Boise, Idaho 83709
(208) 362-3717
www.peregrinefund.org

The Peregrine Fund has participated in conservation projects in more than forty countries. They are best known for the role they played in the restoration of peregrine falcons and bald eagles in the United States.

U.S. Fish and Wildlife Service
Department of the Interior
1849 C St., Rm. 3012
Washington, DC 20240
(202) 208-5634
www.fws.gov

The service is the leading federal agency in the conservation of migratory birds and threatened and endangered species. It operates a program to educate Americans on fish and wildlife resources as well as to assist state governments in the conservation of wildlife.

For Further Reading

Books

Gordon Dee Alcorn, *Owls: An Introduction for the Amateur Naturalist.* New York: Prentice Hall, 1986. A nice book with basic descriptions and natural history of North American owls.

Chris Elphick et al., eds., *The Sibley Guide to Bird Life and Behavior.* New York: Knopf, 2001. A great book on all birds in North America with an excellent description of the two owl families.

Errol Fuller, *Extinct Birds.* New York: Facts On File, 1987. This book covers the birds that have gone extinct in the last hundred years.

Kim Long, *Owls: A Wildlife Handbook.* Boulder, CO: Johnson Books, 1998. This book gives a comprehensive overview of the owls of North America and their habits.

Jemima Parry-Jones, *Eagles and Birds of Prey.* New York: Dorling Kindersley, 1997. This is a good source for the basic features of raptors. It has a section on owls and many good photographs.

Websites

The Barn Owl Centre (www.thebarnowlcentre.co.uk). A website from Great Britain with information on the efforts to save Britain's endangered barn owls.

Owl Pages (www.owlpages.com). A comprehensive list of the owls of the world with photographs and natural history.

Rutgers University Information on Owls (www.rci.rutgers.edu). A wonderful listing of information sources on owls. Includes books and websites.

U.S. Fish and Wildlife (www.endangered.fws.gov). U.S. Fish and Wildlife's information page on currently endangered species in the United States. There is a database as well as links to articles on endangered species.

Works Consulted

Books

John A. Burton, *Owls of the World: Their Evolution, Structure and Ecology.* New York: Dutton, 1973. A very comprehensive book on owl species of the world.

Roger A. Caras, *North American Mammals.* New York: Meredith Press, 1967. Surveys mammals in North America and covers the natural history of a few animals on which owls prey.

James Duncan, ed., *Biology and Conservation of Owls of the Northern Hemisphere.* Winnipeg, Manitoba, CN: USDA Forest Service, 1997. A collection of papers, lectures, and posters presented at the second international owl symposium.

David Fleay, *Nightwatchmen of Bush and Plain.* New York: Taplinger, 1968. Covers the natural history of Australian owls.

Jim Grant, *The Nestbox Book.* Victoria, AU: The Gould League of Victoria, 1997. A book of plans for nest boxes designed for animals of the eucalyptus forest.

Virginia C. Holmgren, *Owls in Folklore and Natural History.* Santa Barbara, CA: Capra Press, 1988. A look at owl history with relationship to humankind.

Claus Konig et al., *Owls: A Guide to the Owls of the World.* New Haven, CT: Yale University Press, 1999. The most comprehensive book on world owl species available.

Jemima Parry-Jones, *Understanding Owls.* Devon, UK: David and Charles, 1998. A book written for educators, breeders, and animal trainers on how to breed, manage, and train owls.

Mike Read and Jake Allsop, *The Barn Owl.* London: Blandford, 1995. A comprehensive book on the barn owl in

England. The authors spent time observing owl families and the book is based on their observations. Their studies are not scientific, but they are interesting and the photography is fantastic.

Richard Standiford et al., *Conserving the California Spotted Owl*. Davis, CA: Wildland Resources Center, 1994. A report published by the Policy Implementation Planning Team for the California spotted owl dealing with their studies and thoughts for conserving this species.

Iain Taylor, *Barn Owls: Predator-Prey Relationships and Conservation*. UK: Cambridge University Press, 1994. A scientific look at barn owls, their predator-prey relationships, and how these relationships apply to their conservation.

Steven Lewis Yaffee, *The Wisdom of the Spotted Owl: Policy Lessons for the New Century*. Washington, DC: Island Press, 1994. This book intensely examines all aspects of the spotted owl debate, covering the subject impartially.

Periodicals

John Cayford and Steve Percival, "Born Free, Die Free," *New Scientist*, February 8, 1992.

Jeffrey P. Cohn, "Sonoran Desert Conservation," *BioScience*, vol. 51, no. 8, 2001.

Shawna J. Dark et al., "The Barred Owl (*Strix varia*) Invasion in California," *The Auk*, vol. 115, no. 1, 1998.

J.L. Gerst, "Endangered and Threatened Wildlife and Plants; Determination Status for the Cactus Ferruginous Pygmy Owl in Arizona," *Fish and Wildlife Service Interior Federal Register*, vol. 62, no. 46, 1997.

Steven M. Goodman and Russell Thorstrom, "The Diet of the Madagascar Red Owl (*Tyto soumagnei*) on the Masoala Peninsula, Madagascar," *Wilson Bulletin*, vol. 110, no. 3, 1998.

Paul C. Hardy and Michael L. Morrison, "Nest Selection by Elf Owls in the Sonoran Desert," *Wilson Bulletin*, vol. 113, no. 1, 2001.

F.A. Richard Hill and Alan Lill, "Density and Total Population Estimates for the Threatened Christmas Island Hawl-Owl (*Ninox natalis*)," *Emu,* vol. 98, 1998.

————, "Diet and Roost Characteristics of the Christmas Island Hawk-Owl (*Ninox natalis*)," *Emu,* vol. 98, 1998.

Bob Holmes, "City Planning for Owls," *National Wildlife,* vol. 36, no. 6, 1998.

William S. LaHaye and R.J. Gutierrez, "Nest Sites and Nesting Habitat of the Northern Spotted Owl in Northwest California," *The Condor,* vol. 101, 1999.

Robert J. Lee and Jon Riley, "Morphology, Plumage, and Habitat of the Newly Described Cinnabar Hawk-Owl from North Sulawesi, Indonesia," *Wilson Bulletin,* vol. 113, no. 1, 2001.

Richard H. Loyn et al., "Modelling Landscape Distributions for Large Forest Owls as Applied to Managing Forests in North-East Victoria, Australia." *Biological Conservation,* vol. 97, 2001.

Jeffrey S. Marks and George F. Barrowclough, "Owls: A Guide to Owls of the World," *The Auk,* July 2001.

Christine A. Moen and R.J. Gutierrez, "California Spotted Owl Habitat Selection in the Central Sierra Nevada," *Journal of Wildlife Management,* vol. 61, no. 4, 1997.

Rick Mooney, "Helping a Heartland Hunter," *National Wildlife,* vol. 26, no. 4, 1988.

C.R. Pavey, "Food of the Powerful Owl (*Ninox strenua*) in Suburban Brisbane, Queensland," *Emu,* vol. 95, 1995.

Roger S. Payne, "Acoustic Location of Prey by Barn Owls (*Tyto alba*)," *Journal of Experimental Biology,* vol. 54, 1971.

Pete Salmansohn, "Plowed Under," *Wildlife Conservation,* vol. 96, November/December 1993.

Martin Shulz, "The Diet of the Powerful Owl (*Ninox strenua*) in the Rockhampton Area," *Emu,* vol. 97, 1997.

Russell Thorstrom, Julian Hart, and Richard T. Watson, "New Record, Ranging Behavior, Vocalization and Food of the Madagascar Red Owl (*Tyto soumagnei*)," *Ibis*, vol. 139, 1997.

R. Thorstrom and R.T. Watson, "Avian Inventory and Key Species of the Masoala Peninsula, Madagascar," *Bird Conservation International,* vol. 7, 1997.

Jared Verner, "Data Needs for Avian Conservation Biology: Have We Avoided Critical Research?" *The Condor,* vol. 94, 1992.

Munir Virani, "Distribution and Population Size of the Sokoke Scops Owl (*Otus ireneae*) in the Arabuko-Sokoke Forest, Kenya." Unpublished paper.

——, "Home Range and Patterns of Sokoke Scops Owl (*Otus ireneae*)," *Ostrich,* vol. 71, nos. 1&2, 2000.

Munir Virani and Richard T. Watson, "Raptors in the East African Tropics and Western Indian Ocean Islands: State of Ecological Knowledge and Conservation Status," *Journal of Raptor Research,* vol. 32, no. 1, 1998.

Jeffery W. Walk et al., "Continuous Nesting of Barn Owls in Illinois," *Wilson Bulletin,* vol. 111, no. 4, 1999.

Guthrie Zimmerman, "Seasonal Variation of Great Horned Owls (*Bubo virginianus*) on Shortgrass Prairie," *American Midland Naturalist,* vol. 136, 1996.

Internet Sources

Associated Press, "Endangered Spotted Owl Faces New Threat from Relative," August 8, 2000. www.cnn.com.

"Christmas Island Hawk-Owl Recovery Outline," *Environment Australia*, October 3, 2000. www.ea.gov.au.

J.A. Dechant et al., "Effects of Management Practices on Grassland Birds: Short-Eared Owl," Northern Prairie Wildlife Research Center, 2001. www.npwrc.usgs.gov.

Tom Hoffman, "Using Barn Owls for Rodent Control," Bio-Diversity Products, 1998. www.members.tripod.com.

John Roach, "Harry Potter Owl Scenes Alarm Animal Advocates," *National Geographic News*, November 16, 2001. http://news.nationalgeographic.com.

Mykola Rud, "Eagle Owl (*Bubo bubo*)," *The Naturalist,* 2001. http://proeco.visti.net.

Peter Spinks, "Island Showdown: Crazy Ants v. Christmas Crabs," *The Age,* March 26, 1999. www.theage.com.

John Young, "Masked Owl Population Saved from Brink of Extinction," Ray Smith Productions, 1997. www.raysp.com.

John Zarrella, "Growers Find Barn Owls Protect Their Crops," *CNN Interactive*, June 10, 1997. http://europe.cnn.com.

Websites

Barn Owl Headquarters (www.members.tripod.com/tommy51). A great website on the natural history of barn owls and their usefulness as pest controllers. There are many good links on this site as well.

Protect the Sonoran Desert (www.sonorandesert.org). On this website you will find great information on the Sonoran Desert Project as well as some ways to live on and conserve desert habitat.

Sweet Home On-Line (www.sweet-home.or.us). This website gives the history and future plans of the small logging town of Sweet Home, which was greatly affected by the spotted owl controversy.

Index

rabbits, 67
rain forests, 26–31, 80
ranches, 35
rictal bristles, 17, 24
Roach, John, 54
rodenticides, 49, 55–56, 60
rods, 17–18
Rud, Mykola, 46
Russia, 46

Santa Clara, 82
Saskatchewan, 79
sclerotic ring, 15–16
Second International Symposium on the Biology and Conservation of Owls, 49
Shakespeare, William, 43
Shoesmith, Merlin, 49–50
short-eared owl, 34, 61
snowy owl, 54
Sokoke scops owl, 27–32
Sokoke Scops Owl Project, 32
Sonoran Desert Project, 88–89
Sonoran Desert Protection Plan, 77
soup, 44
sparrows, 66
spotted owl, 29, 47–48, 62–63, 68, 76–77
squirrels, 64
starlings, 66
starvation, 70
Strigidae family, 10–11
Strigiformes, 10, 24
Sulawesi, 13
Sunshine, 49
sustainable harvests, 80–81

Sweet Home, 48
symbiotic relationships, 64–65

Tanzania, 28
Taylor, Iain, 56, 73, 81
thermoregulation, 24
Thiollay, J.M., 31
Thurston, Jenny, 54
traffic, 57–58
Tucson, 36–37, 89
Tytonidae family, 10

Ukraine, 46
understory, 26
United Kingdom, 54
U.S. Fish and Wildlife Service, 24–25, 48, 53, 89
U.S. Forest Service, 48
Usambara Mountains, 28

Victoria, Australia, 40–41
Virani, Munir, 27, 30, 32, 85
voles, 33–34, 58–61, 75, 77–78
vulnerable species, 22

Warfarin, 56
water, 76–77
water troughs, 56
weasels, 67
weather, 70–73
Western Australia, 39–40
whooping cough, 44
wings, 11–13, 20
witches, 43
woodpeckers, 64–65

zoos, 49

Picture Credits

About the Author

Rebecca O'Connor is a professional animal trainer who resides in southern California. She has a degree in creative writing and a passion for raptors, especially ones that inhabit the dark of the night.